Rondo Soccer Drills

Chest Dugger

Table Of Contents

ABOUT THE AUTHOR

Chest Dugger is a soccer fan, former professional and coach, looking to share his knowledge. Enjoy this book and several others that he has written.

Free Gift Included

As part of our dedication to help you succeed in your career, we have sent you a free soccer drills worksheet, known as the "Soccer Training Work Sheet" drill sheet. The worksheet is a list of drills that you can use to improve your game and a methodology to track your performance on these drills on a day-to-day basis. We want to get you to the next level.

Click on the link below to get your free drills worksheet.

https://soccertrainingabiprod.gr8.com/

DISCLAIMER

Introduction

Rondos transformed soccer. Rondos helped turn the Spanish national team into the best in the world. The system behind Rondos was the beating heart of the brilliant Barcelona teams, which dominated Europe for a decade from 2005. They made soccer even more exciting to watch, improving players' technical ability and creating a proper, total football (in the European sense) game. Their approach was reminiscent of the fantastic Ajax team of the 1970s and the great Dutch teams of that era. They led to the excitement of the high press and the thrilling soccer, which follows when the press is defeated.

They proved the benefit of technique over physical prowess.

So, what is this miracle of the training pitch which has so transformed the game of soccer? The beauty of the rondo is its simplicity. It is a drill where the objective is to retain possession. As rondo drills become more complex, this aim might develop. It might be about keeping possession in transition or maintaining possession to create a goal-scoring opportunity. However, at its heart is the objective of one side keeping hold of the ball.

A second key element of a rondo is that the sides are uneven. One team has extra players. It can take a form as exaggerated as 10 v 1, or as close as 5 v 4. However, the point is that some pressure is applied, but not so much as to make the drill difficult to perfect. Thus, confidence grows, and in turn, touch and vision.

A rondo is usually a drill that takes place in a limited space; typically a circle, square or rectangular grid. Thus first and second touches are perfected because there is not much time to take many touches.

Finally, and crucially, rondos are drills that are fast and fun. They involve lots of touches for the players in possession and a real sense of achievement on the rare occasions that the smaller side actually wins back the ball.

So simple. Yet so effective.

This coaching book celebrates the rondo and offers drills, tactics, and coaching techniques to help soccer players at any level, from the unbounded enthusiasm of Under 6s to the worldly view of veteran teams. From the pub side who turn out on a Sunday morning, cooked breakfast weighing heavily on their hangover-infused stomachs to the champion youth team of the region.

We can all improve as coaches, just as we can all improve as players. The rondo is the system that enables progress to happen more quickly and efficiently than any other soccer coaching strategy.

Key to Diagrams

Many of the following 100 drills, tactics and techniques include diagrams. They have been used to help with clarity in understanding the operation of the drills. In these:

Black Circle = Defender

White Circle = Attacker (Team in Possession)

Black/White Circle with a G inside = Goalkeeper

Circles with other letters or numbers – Players with clarifications

Grey Circle = Extra team players if needed

Small Grey Circle = Ball

Thin Black Line = Movement of the Ball in a Pass or Shot

Thick White Line = Movement of an Attacker

Thick Black Line = Movement of a Defender

White Square or Circle (outline) = Grid / Drill Area

Grey Line = Ball being Dribbled

Dashed Grey Line = Pass or Shot after Change of Possession

There are specific explanations of symbols by some drills, and they are not drawn to scale.

The Philosophy Behind Rondo

There is nothing quite like seeing the team we coach play well. Winning is important, of course, although we know these days that it is not as important as perhaps, we once thought it was. But playing well, utilizing those skills and techniques we practised in training. That provides another level of satisfaction altogether.

When one achieves that high degree of precision on the pitch, there is a good chance that it has resulted from the coach and their team working hard on rondo-type drills. Rondos took the professional world by storm. Like many successful trends, they found their place, and forward-thinking coaches embedded the principles behind them, and moved them on further still. As is the case with so much best practice in all kinds of sports, gradually, those principles filtered down to the grassroots game. These days the best amateur and youth coaches employ rondo drills in their coaching programs.

The result is improvement in technique, teamwork, decision-making, communication, and skill levels. Fundamentally, rondos take the critical traits of a good soccer player and move them up to a higher standard. At the same time, they teach and embed those traits in players we might class as less able or less experienced.

One (Tactic): Keep it tight

A vital principle of a rondo is that it takes place in limited space. Of course, an Under-8s team will not have the same level of touch as an adult side, at least not for a while. But even with the youngest soccer players, that crucial skill will come surprisingly quickly with effective coaching. So, while there must be some attention paid to the level of the players undertaking any particular drill, it is key that space is controlled.

With lots of time and plenty of space, average players can hide deficiencies in touch and decision-making. Under pressure, they cannot. Hence, in every drill that follows, we shorten the space available as soon as skill levels merit this. While we can offer guides, it is down to the coach's skill to determine the best challenge level for their team, taking into account skills, age, and experience.

Dutch Dream, Spanish Reality

When Johan Cruyff died of cancer, far too young at just 68, not only was soccer forced to say goodbye to one of its greats, but the entire sports loving world was made to mourn. The Dutch FA said at the time the lynchpin of its great teams of the 1970s was the 'greatest Dutch footballer of all time, and one of the world's best ever.' There is no overstatement in that. It was Cruyff who held the mantle of being the world's finest player in the period between the two who are probably the very greatest of all time; Pele and Maradona. Unlike these South American geniuses, Cruyff never managed to secure the greatest honour of all – winning the World Cup – but that could not detract from his astonishing brilliance. On three occasions he was crowned European footballer of the year – it should have been more. He won three consecutive European Cups with that astonishing Ajax team of the early 1970s which dominated European football and won their own league, the Eredivisie, no less than eight times. He led his national side to the 1974 World Cup final. Maybe that elusive World Cup winner's medal would have graced his own extensive trophy cabinet had not a kidnapping attempt persuaded him to miss the 1978 tournament where, even without him, the Dutch side reached the final once more.

But if it is as a player that Cruyff is best remembered, his contribution to soccer in his role as a coach cannot be underestimated. Because it is Johan Cruyff who is credited with inventing the rondo.

Maybe 'inventing' is too strong a term. Certainly, any older readers will recall their own childhood days on school and club pitches, the coach telling them to get a ball, form up as a three or four, and play 'piggy in the middle' to warm up. That would be prior to the start of the session proper, when the coach would split his players, with the attackers learning to kick the ball and the defense to kick the opposition. But it was Cruyff, through the influence of the Dutch system of total football, who formalised the rondo, and realised that it could improve all aspects of a player's game bar, perhaps, shooting.

In 2012 Stan Baker published 'Our Competition is the World', an excellent introduction to the world of youth soccer coaching, and also a fine read in itself. In it Cruyff says: 'Everything that goes on in a match, except shooting, you can do in a rondo. The competitive aspect, fighting to make space, what to do when in possession and what to do when you haven't got the ball, how to play 'one touch' soccer, how to counteract the tight marking and how to win the ball back.' A pretty glowing assessment of the rondo, we have to say.

Xavi Hernandez was a key figure in perhaps the greatest Barcelona team ever, the one of the mid-2000s to the mid-2010s to which we must constantly refer. He spoke to the Guardian newspaper in 2011 and explained the significance of Cruyff's influence on the philosophy of the club. 'Some youth academies worry about winning,' he said. 'We (Barcelona) worry about education. You see a kid who lifts his head up, who plays the pass first time, pum, and you think "Yep, he'll do." Bring him in, coach him. Our model was imposed by Cruyff: it's an Ajax model. It's all about rondos. Rondo, rondo, rondo. Every. Single. Day. It's the best exercise there is. You learn responsibility and not to lose the ball. If you lose the ball, you go in the middle. Pum-pum-pum-pum, always one touch. If you go in the middle, it's humiliating, the rest applaud and laugh at you.'

It was around this time, 2011, that the rest of the world began to wake up to what Barcelona were doing. Physically, they were a small team. (Although, as any watcher could observe, the masters of the nudge off the ball). As their coach, the great Pep Guardiola, said: 'Without the ball we are a horrible team. So, we need the ball.' That meant keeping the ball once they had it. They did so through their soccer, which transferred itself to the great Spanish national sides of that era and was often described as tika taka football. Lots of short, one touch passing; precise, incisive, incredible passing allied to astonishingly accurate and consistent decision making. It was a system of play that could only be achieved through regular and thorough drilling.

Two (Coaching Strategy): When adopting a philosophy based on the rondo, it is essential to commit fully to it

It is the familiarity with teammates which is a key element of the rondo. Therefore, it is a philosophy, or coaching system (the two are interchangeable here) to which a coach must fully commit. To achieve maximum benefit, rondos must become the dominant system of drills and practices which underpin training sessions.

The Ultimate Accolade

To return to 2011. It is the Champions League final. Wembley Stadium. Even in the warm up, the crowd and watching millions on TV are agape at the speed and skill of the Barcelona players' touch. On the pitch, Manchester United, an extremely powerful side themselves, are torn apart. They cannot get near to the opposition. The final result, 3-1 to the Spanish masters, does not reflect their level of domination. The Manchester United manager, Sir Alex Ferguson, can only be honest in his post-match interview, despite his inevitable disappointment.

'We were well beaten,' he admitted. 'There is no other way to address the situation. They do mesmerize you with their passing. They're the best in Europe, no question about that. In my time as a manager, I would say they're the best team we've faced. Everyone acknowledges that and I accept that.'

The multiple trophy winning Scot went on to say: 'It's not easy when you've been well beaten like that to think another way. No one has given us a hiding like that. It's a great moment for them. They deserve it because they play the right way and enjoy their football.'

Not every young girl and boy starting out on their soccer playing career is going to become a top flight professional. Not every seasoned club player is going to become a new man or a revitalised player thanks to the introduction of rondos. But they are going to become better at soccer if their club adopts a rondo-based philosophy. Yet…it won't happen overnight.

Three (Coaching Strategy): Removing Fear

Rondos are typically quite simple. There is rarely much setting up of equipment. Mostly, just a grid is needed, and a ball. Usually, the basis of the drill is about two things. For the larger, weighted, team it is about keeping possession. For the smaller sided opponents, it is about ending that possession. Usually, and for most of the time, the side with the extra players will dominate.

However, the lack of space which characterises rondos adds pressure and leads to mistakes. It is how the coach reacts to those mistakes, and how he or she creates the atmosphere under which their players react which is key to the success of the rondo. As can be seen from Xavi's comments above, and to be honest was abundantly obvious from watching the Barcelona team in which he played, enjoyment was a key element of their soccer. Players enjoy soccer when they can perform without fear. When they are prepared to make mistakes because they are prepared to try to do something special.

That must be encouraged. When something goes wrong, and the player moves from being in the larger, possession-based group to the small defensive one, that must be seen as an opportunity to learn new skills. Total football. Everybody defends. Everybody attacks. Everybody has a good touch. Everybody is allowed to express themselves. Total football. Like the Netherlands, like Ajax, like Barcelona. Therefore, errors must be welcomed, not criticised. Only when mistakes are made can players improve. Everything must be fun; fear must be eliminated. That is true whether we are coach of an Under

Seven group of kids taking their first steps on the playing fields, or a vets' team who have seen it all and done it all. Removing fear can be hard, because, for a long time, coaching was based on criticism. Remember the days when to be a defender meant you could not cross the half-way line? Hopefully not, but many of we readers will.

When the mindset among the entire squad is that playing soccer equates to having fun, and rondos are a chance to experiment, to take risks and to learn the effectiveness of simplicity, they work. Patience is needed to achieve this. And repetition.

Here are the key points from the chapter:

- Rondo drills will help players to develop:
  - ➢ Improved first touch.
  - ➢ Improved passing.
  - ➢ Improved team work and understanding.
  - ➢ Improved communication.
  - ➢ Improved tactical awareness...
  - ➢ Improved defense...
- In order to be at their most effective, repetition is required.
- A rondo philosophy needs total commitment to the system.

• Players must play without fear, because they must enjoy their soccer in order to make the most progress

In the next chapter we will turn our attention to a more detailed analysis of the benefits that rondo drills can deliver.

The Benefits of Rondo Drills

What makes a good training session? And what makes a bad one?

Complex questions with straightforward answers. The best sessions are marked by the following:

• Individual progress of all players. This might include any or all from improved technique, the acquisition of new skills, stronger understanding of tactics, improved fitness, better communication and improved team work skills.

• Team progress. This might include improvements of the whole squad in their team play and tactics, or units within the team, such as the defense or the midfield. Although, whilst we would advocate some work on units within the team, the modern game requires all players to have a good touch, accurate passing and the ability to defend. By all players, we definitely include the goalkeeper. The modern game is developing in a way whereby the 'keeper, as the spare player, is often the starting point of an attack.

• Satisfaction of individual and team needs. By this, we mean that the coach has identified, and addressed, priorities for the development of the team and the individuals who form it.

- Players understanding what they are seeking to achieve, and why.

- An enjoyable time. This means a focus on fun and action, with minimal talking or standing still. This is especially important with younger age groups, whose concentration may be short and who cannot often take in complex and long-winded information. (Let us be honest, we would all rather be playing than listening…)

Conversely, a bad session will be typified by lots of standing around from the players, even if they are listening to the coach's words of wisdom. A lack of focus on key skills or techniques, and a lack of organisation. A lack of attention to both details and individuals completes the catalogue of bad coaching techniques.

Yet another reason as to why rondos make an excellent system to use in training sessions is that they address the features of a positive session and are usually the opposite of the features of a weak session.

Take a look at the section headings below. Overwhelmingly, they are about action and activity, not listening or passivity. Let us focus in more detail on the key benefits of using a rondo based coaching philosophy, along with some practical drills which can help to deliver success. Please refer back to the introduction for a key to the symbols used in the diagrams.

Touch

Rondo drills create pressure. There is always an opposition to chase down a pass, to pick up on any mis-control. At the same time, that pressure is not as intense as in an equal sided practice or game, where each player can have their own opponent or marker. Therefore, touch improves through this significant but not overwhelming pressure.

Further, Rondos are naturally small sided. They are also fast. Therefore, players receive many touches during a session, so there is plenty of opportunity to improve that touch.

Four (Drill): Developing First Touch

Aim: Improve first touch

Objectives:

- Keep possession by passing across a grid.
- Stop the ball in the correct body position to make the next pass.

- Keep possession by passing with one or two touches.
- Move to support a teammate.

Organisation:

- 15 x 15 metre grid. (This can be larger or smaller depending on the skill level of the players.)
- 5 v 2 players.
- One attacker on each side of the grid, one in the middle. Two defenders in the grid. Players inside the grid cannot leave it.

Operation of Drill:

- Play begins with one player passing to any of their teammates.
- That player then passes to another teammate, or back to the original passer.
- Defenders try to intercept pass, win the ball after the first touch or force a pass that goes beyond a teammate.
- When possession is lost, the pressing defender swaps positions with the attacker who has given away possession.

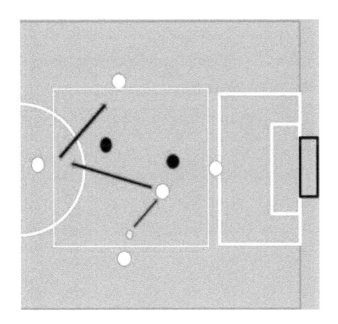

Key Skills:

- Players cushion the ball on receipt, if using two touches.
- Receive the ball on the half turn to protect the ball.
- Shift the ball with a first touch to the direction of the next pass.
- Head over the ball, arms for balance.
- Pass firmly, with the instep, with either first or second touch.

- Be prepared to encourage risk taking with back heels, one touch Cruyff style turns, reverse passes and passing with the outside of the foot.
- Teammates are mobile all of the time to give options for the pass.
- Teammates anticipate movement of the defense to give options for the pass.
- Defense works as a unit to restrict passing options and create pressure.

Development:

- Allow interchanging of attacking players in the grid to increase movement and develop communication.
- Allow multiple attacking players inside the grid, again to improve movement.
- Allow multiple players in the grid but add the rule that any pass from outside the grid must be made into the grid. This will put more pressure on the first touch of these players.

Movement

The speed of a rondo helps players to understand the importance of movement, both in receiving the ball and in running off the ball to create space for others. Defensive players understand the importance of positional play, since attempting one v one tackling, or relying just on superior speed will never stand up to the pressure of being outnumbered, whilst the extra space teammates have means that runs made are likely to get rewarded.

The following drill is an excellent one for improving movement for both strikers and defenders. For a rondo style drill, it comprises of a lot of players, which means also that without good movement, strikers will be easily marked out of the game, whilst if they do make effective runs, they have enough teammates to be fed the ball.

Five (Drill): Squad Ahoy

Aims: Make good runs to get into goal scoring positions.

Objectives:

- Make good defensive and offensive movement to limit/create space.
- Communicate.
- Use width to create space.
- Score goals.

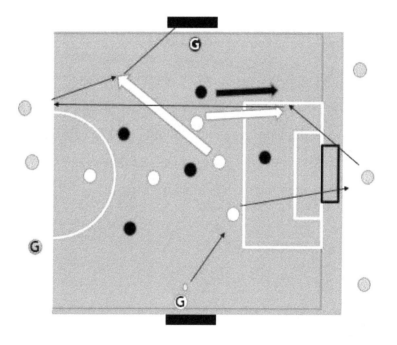

Organisation:

- 6 a side pitch or half full pitch, goal at each end.
- Three teams of ideally six players including goalkeeper. The drill work with seven a side or five a side as well.
- Two sides play a match, the third side are positioned around the outside of the playing area, approximately 2 m back from the side-lines.
- The players on the 3rd side are allowed two touches. They are always on the side of the team who just passed to them. They may not enter the field of play.
- Players on the other teams are not allowed outside the field of play. Thereby, there is no pressure on the 'outside' team.

Operation of Drill:

- Play begins with the goalkeeper passing to a teammate. The teammate must pass to an outside player.
- At that point the game becomes live. The defensive team are allowed to challenge for the ball once it comes back into play and attempts at goal can be made.

- After a maximum of THREE internal passes from within the pitch, if no attempt at goal has taken place, a pass to one of the outside players must take place.
- Swap the outside team every three to five minutes, or after every third shot at goal.

Key Skills:

- Players make runs into space when a pass to the outside is made.
- Players communicate their runs.
- Players attempt to develop a 'picture' of the game, by anticipating how a move will develop.

Development:

- Change the positioning of the outside team to two along each side, and one behind each by-line.
- Limit the number of touches to all players, reducing to one or two depending on their ability levels.

Passing

After first touch, probably the biggest benefit of a rondo lies with the improvement it induces in passing. Players become more adept at one touch passing, because they often need to employ it as they are pressured by the opposition. That they will always have a teammate in space, because of their overload of players, encourages them to try passing at different angles and with different parts of the foot, since they are likely to be rewarded with success. Again, the very nature of a rondo, with its limited space, encourages short rather than long passing. We are not arguing that there is no place in the game for the long pass. As a way of mixing up tactics, of providing a surprise element, it is an especially important skill to acquire.

However, we can see in the current game just how the predominance of rondo drills at the highest levels has developed tactics. Now, most of the time, teams will aim to keep possession by playing out from the back, using their keeper as the spare player.

That defenders and the keeper must be confident and capable on the ball can only be good for the game at the highest levels, and for enjoyment of players at youth level. They can be very few players indeed who do not enjoy trying a bit of skill or a first-time pass, and thanks to rondos they have both the technique to do so, and the playing strategies which allow this.

Of course, soccer adapts. The response to the rondo initiated playing out from the back is the high press, whereby the aim is to win possession high up the pitch, and because the high press features several players, have teammates already on hand ready to exploit the transition. In turn, the use of the occasional long ball, or the damage caused when the press is beaten, has turned the high press into a more cautiously used tactic. It will be fascinating to see where top coaches take this aspect of the game next.

However, we digress. The following drill is a very simple but very effective one to improve passing.

Six (Drill): Multiple Passes

Aim: Make 30 passes.

Objectives:

- Make multiple one or two touch passes.
- Defenders shadow passing, communicating and working together to exploit the situation where control begins to be lost.

Organisation:

- 10 x 10 metre grid (This can be larger or smaller depending on the skill level of the players. Coaches of more advanced teams can use the drill to both practice what is, for them, the optimal passing length, or address a weakness, such as in short passing.)
- The grid could also be a circle, such as the centre circle, or even a rectangle to practice passes of different lengths.
- 8 v 2 players.
- Players pass across the grid, with the coach setting the number of touches allowed.

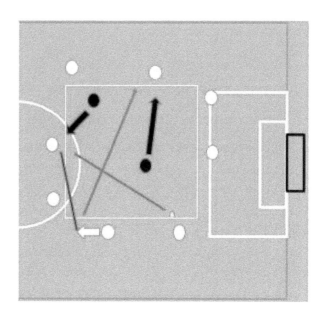

Operation of Drill:

- The attacking team spread around the outside of the grid.
- Two defenders are in the middle, attempting to intercept the ball or force a misplaced pass.
- Attackers pass across the grid. They can pass to any teammate provide the ball goes into the grid at some point. They cannot simply pass around the outside.
- When possession is lost, the player last in possession, and the person who passed to him or her, swaps with the defender.

- The coach sets a target, say twenty or thirty passes, as a goal.

Key Skills:

- First touch.
- Firm passing, along the ground.
- Communication.
- Developing confidence with different types of pass.
- Defense works together to force an error.
- Defense communicates and pounces when a pass leaves the ground, when a first touch is weak, or a pass lacks accuracy. It is often on the subsequent pass that possession will be lost.

Development:

- Introduce a bit of fun if the age, confidence and personality of the players allows it. At professional levels, a lot of the pleasure of this drill was the gentle banter when the passing target was reached. As long as it is controlled, that is fine. It encourages the defense to work harder.
- Limit touches.

- Make the grid smaller.

Communication

We have already seen that the speed of a rondo emphasises the importance of communication. Simply, without help from teammates, a player receiving the ball will not get a full picture of what is going on around her.

Seven (Coaching Strategy): Communication List

Familiarity breeds competence and, in turn, success. Develop a series of calls which are common to the team, providing that extra second of thinking time for players in possession.

Eight (Drill): No Time to Talk

This is not a rondo drill as such but is useful for making the point that communication is crucial in soccer. It can be turned, riskily, into a rondo by closely weighting the teams, then allowing the smaller side to talk. That should even up matters, although a bit of jeopardy is provided if it goes wrong! We don't want our players to think that being quiet is the key to success!

Aim: Understand the Importance of Communication.

Objectives:

- Play a normal game.
- No talking. No gestures,

Organisation:

- 6 a side. Short game, say 10 minutes.

Operation of Drill:

- Any communication, talking or gesturing, results in a free kick to the opposition.

Key Skills:

- The drill is really a negative one, which seeks to demonstrate the difficulty of playing without communication.

- It can, however, help defenders to be extra careful when protecting the ball if they get possession.

Development:

- Get even tougher by taking off for one minute any player who communicates.
- Follow up with a brief plenary about the problems players faced without communication.
- Also see if any found advantages, such as not feeling pressured. This may help coaches to improve the QUALITY of communication.

Teamwork

This follows neatly on from communication. The tight spaces of rondo drills encourage teamwork.

Nine (Coaching Strategy): Knowing our Job

We do not advocate a lot of talking during training sessions. More is learned by doing than listening. However, a brief follow-up to a drill can be useful, as long as that discussion moves at pace. Find out what works for players about the drill, which skills or techniques they feel they need to practise. Such discussions lend themselves to coaches having the opportunity of stressing the multiple roles of players. Particularly those which lie outside of playing the ball. Support, communication, encouragement, making runs and so forth. Even with experienced players, knowing one's job makes you a better player.

Good coaches can build an opportunity to remind players of their responsibilities into a coaching session, planning on how to direct discussion around to it so the advice seems appropriate and well timed, rather than dictatorial or critical.

Ten (Drill): Teamwork support

This drill stresses the importance of supporting teammates when they are in danger of losing the ball.

Aim: React to pressure to support player with ball.

Objectives:

- Recognise when a player is under pressure, and close to give support.
- Ensure that despite change of position, body shape is still correct to receive the ball.
- Recognise when control is regained.

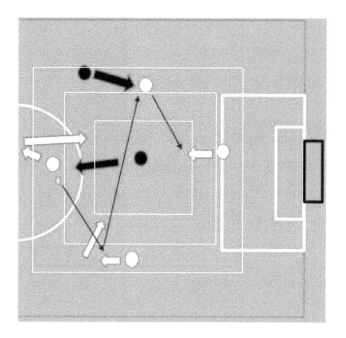

Organisation:

- Three grids, the largest 15 x 15 m, one of 10 x 10 m and one of 8 x 8 m, inside each other.
- 4 v 2 players.

- One attacker on each side of the 10m grid, one defender in the middle. The other defender can move to anywhere on the 15m grid.

Operation of Drill:

- Normal one or two touch passing around the grid. Inside defender pressures.
- At a stage of their choosing, the outside defender moves to pressure the player receiving the ball. They will probably be coming from behind.
- Teammates of the attacker under pressure give a warning.
- Teammates move either to the smaller, 8m grid, to offer an easier pass, or back to the 15m grid to give more space for the pass.
- Once control is regained, the defenders swap positions, and the attackers move back to the middle, 10m grid.

Key Skills:

- Players concentrate on the changing situation of pressure on the ball.
- Players communicate effectively.

- Players make decisions regarding whether to close in for support or move out for support.
- Players choose when control is regained.
- Teammates anticipate movement of defense to give options for the pass.
- Defense works as a unit to restrict passing options and create pressure.

Development:

- Discuss players' decision making after the drill. (Keep discussions brief but bring out key points.)
- Increase the teams to 5 v 3, to place additional pressure on the ball.

Defense

Certainly, the rondo is highly effective at improving the skills and techniques associated with offensive play. But they also help defenders to become more effective at their own game. In fact, that is not the absolute truth. What a rondo does, to bring about defensive improvement, is teach all players the importance of, as well as the challenges inherent within, defending.

Transition

Rondos are based around keeping possession. They are therefore extremely useful at teaching teams to utilise any possession that is won. We will look at the high press in a later chapter, but the tip and drill below are particularly important in a sport where possession is increasingly retained for long periods.

Eleven (Coaching Strategy): The Importance of Transition

Try to include at least one specific drill in each session which focuses on the transition stage of soccer. Remember to work on defensive tactics as well as offensive.

Twelve (Tactics): Teaching Tactics – the value of technology

Another tip is for coaches to build up a library of video clips to share with the team. We are looking specifically at transition now, but the point is valid for whichever tactic a team is trying to grasp. Seeing it in action, then attempting to replicate what a professional outfit has achieved is an effective teaching tool.

Thirteen (Drill): Transition Rondo

Aim: Change tactical formation on transition

Objectives:

- Work collectively to keep and win back possession.
- Score points for making five passes without interception.
- Change tactically and numerically on transition, replicating the advance of support players in a match situation.

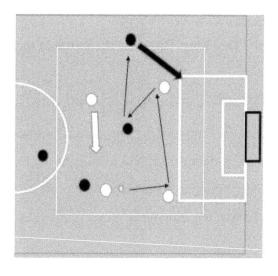

Organisation:

- Grid. 10 x 10m is a good starting point, but this drill can be used with anything from medium sized groups to quite large ones. The size of the grid will expand depending on numbers and the skill levels of the players.
- 4 v 4 and up to 8 v 8 players.
- Divide players into two even teams.

Operation of Drill:

- Team in possession has all players in the grid.
- Team out of possession has two players out of the grid along separate lines of the grid.
- Team in possession attempt to string together five passes. If they do so, they score a point.
- Team out of possession try to win the ball. However, they are only judged to have completed transition when they win the ball and pass it to one of their outside players.
- At this point, two of the team who have just lost possession move to the outside of the grid, whilst their opponents come back into the grid, and their team begins their attempt to make five passes from that point.

Key Skills:

- Deciding which players will move out of the grid when possession is judged to have been lost.
- Players moving into the grid take up good positions since they are likely to be the 'spare' player on this transition.
- Defense tries to get into good pressuring position, seeking to move to intercept or tackle when they spot a wayward pass, or the ball leaves the ground.
- Team in possession seek to support players closely when they are struggling to maintain control and find space when the player on the ball has time.

Development:

- Since the point scoring objective is to make successive passes, there is no specific need to impose limited touches. However, the coach can do so to force the team in possession to play the ball more quickly, something especially important during the transition phase of a match.
- Increase the number of players outside of the grid from 2 to 3.

Fitness

Rondo drills typically take place in small areas, which would appear to negate against their benefit for fitness. However, they encourage fast movement and fast thinking, both of which help to generate that physical and mental fitness coaches seek in their teams.

The following drill can be used with any age group, although adults might prefer a different 'body drop'. It works particularly well with younger players, however.

Fourteen (Drill): Fitness Rondo

Aims: Improve physical fitness and mental agility.

Objectives:

- Keep possession by passing across a grid.
- Think quickly about the next pass.
- Improve physical fitness with different body movements.

Organisation:

- Small grid to encourage fast action. No larger than 10 x 10 m.
- 4 v 1 players, attackers on outside, defender inside grid.

Operation of Drill:

- Drill operates as a normal 4 v 1 grid drill, with the player in the middle attempting to win possession or force a wayward pass.
- When a player makes a pass, they must fall flat to the ground on their stomach, effectively preventing a reverse pass to them.
- The 'body fall' helps to develop their physical fitness since they must move quickly to get back into the game. It is particularly useful for defenders and goalkeepers who must get to their feet rapidly after going to ground.
- Mental agility is developed as passers have to consider quickly which of their teammates are available at that moment.

- The defender can work tactically to close off the simple pass, since he or she knows one of their opponents is temporarily out of the game.
- When possession is lost, the pressing defender swaps positions with the attacker who has played the pass which has given away possession.

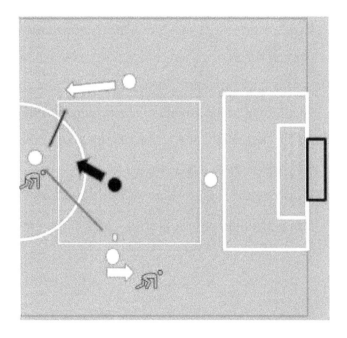

Key Skills:

- Encourage fast passing with one or two touches.
- Encourage communication.

Development:

- With young children, who enjoy the silliness of such, change the body fall position regularly. For example, 'lie on your back', 'sit on your bottom', 'touch the ground with your head'.
- Place four cones each 5m back from the lines of the grid. Rather than fall, players must sprint around the cone after passing before they can re-join the game. Adults and older youths might find this fitness technique more applicable than falling to the ground. (Then again, watching soccer on TV these days, and witnessing the ease and regularity with which many professionals seem to hit the deck following the slightest contact, perhaps adults might decide that falling over is an essential skill to master! ☺)

Fifteen (Coaching Strategy): Soccer is also called Football. The Clue is in the Second Syllable

A notable change in training strategies of recent years is that 'going for a run' has fallen out of fashion and fitness training using a ball has grown in popularity. This makes sense. Fitness is a crucial attribute of any soccer player but can be achieved while other skills are developed with a ball at feet.

Rondo drills take this combination of fitness training along with skill and technique development to a high level.

Fun

Lastly, but most importantly, in this chapter we look at the crucial role of 'fun' in soccer. Rondo drills are fun. The overloading of one team helps to deliver success, which all players enjoy. They help to offer challenge, which is mentally stimulating, and they encourage fast movement and experimentation, which players find engaging.

However, we can take this to higher levels. The following drill encourages experimentation, concentration and skill development. It is likely to go wrong quite often, and when that happens, we encourage our players to smile at their mistake.

Sixteen (Drill): Dumb Ways to Pass

Aim: Encourage players to experiment with different types of pass.

Objectives:

- Keep possession by passing across a grid.
- Focus on how teammates are passing.
- Attempt to pass in different ways.

Organisation:

- 10 x 10 m grid
- 4 v 1 players

Operation of Drill:

- This is a normal pass across the grid rondo drill.

- No two consecutive passes can be the same. For example, an instep pass must be followed by a backheel, or a pass with the outside of the foot.
- Defenders try to intercept the pass, win the ball after the first touch or force a pass that goes beyond a teammate.
- When possession is lost, the pressing defender swaps positions with the attacker who has given away possession.

Key Skills:

- Players must concentrate on what their teammates are doing.
- Learn different ways of passing.
- Laugh a lot!

Development:

- Try different rules. For example, left foot pass followed by a right foot pass. Or must use one touch followed by must use two touch.

Seventeen (Coaching Strategy): Make Sessions Fun

If we look back to some of the comments of professionals, players at the top of their game, as they explain how much they enjoyed rondo drills, we can take away a really important lesson. If fun is so valued by these players, earning millions to perform their profession, then it becomes even more so for youth players, and amateurs turning out because they want to.

We all wish to become the best coach we can be. Perhaps there is an easy way to achieve this. *The best coaches allow their players to enjoy their soccer. Because, when we have fun, we learn.*

The key points from this chapter are:

- Rondo style drills can be employed to help the development of almost all aspects of soccer.
- Basic drills are easily adapted to achieve different aims.
- Rondos are fun, and fun is at the heart of soccer.

A Short message from the Author:

Hey, are you enjoying the book? I'd love to hear your thoughts!

Many readers do not know how hard reviews are to come by, and how much they help an author.

I would be incredibly thankful if you could take just 60 seconds to write a brief review on Amazon, even if it's just a few sentences!

Browse to the product page and leave a review as shown below.

Thank you for taking the time to share your thoughts!

Your review will genuinely make a difference for me and help gain exposure for my work.

Soccer Warm Up Rondos

Why warm up before a game? And why cool down after a training session? In the past, it is probably fair to say that we warmed up because of some vague notion that it prevented injury. This is true, to an extent, but warming up will provide far more benefit than this. We cooled down at the end…with a cold beer. Or if we were too young for that, by sharing the exploits of the session just gone from the back of the car. Certainly, that involved exercise, but of the jaw rather than the muscles we had just pushed to their limits.

Science educates, and we know now that there are very important physiological reasons for warming up. And let us not forget, cooling down. Our warm ups should focus of the muscles we are about to use in the match ahead, or the training session which will follow. Given our sport is soccer, the probability is that we will be using most of our body's muscles, so we all need a good warm up. The aim is to use this mild exercise to stimulate blood flow to the muscles. This in turn increases oxygen levels in our soft tissues and removes carbon dioxide. The muscles do actually warm up, so the name we give to this exercise is a good one…

And it gets better. As our muscles warm up oxygen starts to separate from our haemoglobin, the fluid which transports that oxygen. As a result, our muscles become less viscous, and therefore become both more sensitive to the demands we put on them, and the speed with which they react. Simply, warming up allows our brain to connect more quickly to our muscles. We become more effective players as a result of warming up.

However, as we said earlier, soccer involves using most of the muscles in the body; what better way, then, to warm up than with a soccer related drill? Because rondos are fast paced, but do not over pressurise the physical elements of our body, they make perfect warm up and cool down exercises.

The rondos used for these purposes need to be very simple, and not require much setting up. Particularly at the beginning of a session, when players are likely to arrive at different times. The session starts well if those players who arrive promptly are immediately involved in activity. Soon, they will learn to start the warm up on their own.

Many of us will have seen that these five minutes as the players arrive can be wasted. Players, adults as well as kids, go off and practise shooting, or some other similar activity which places stress on unwarmed muscles. Shooting involves only the person taking the shot and perhaps a goalkeeper. It is a dreadful warm up activity, possibly even worse than the 'stand around and chat' start which promises a less than perfect session ahead. At least it is hard to get injured when talking!

Eighteen (Coaching Strategy): The Importance of Cooling Down – a Club Philosophy

Explaining the importance of this vital component of any type of soccer session is hard enough with adults, let alone young players. Put simply, when we exercise our blood vessels expand. When we stop exercising, our heart rate falls and we pump the blood through our bodies less vigorously, resulting in blood pooling in those expanded blood vessels. Gravity dictates that the excess blood mainly ends up in our legs.

This can increase the risk of injury, slow the speed of recovery and increase soreness the following day. By carrying out gentle exercise after a hard game or training session, we allow the blood, and therefore oxygen, to be pumped around the body and give our blood vessels time to spring back to their normal state. Oxygen aids muscle recovery, and so the cool down is vitally important.

But very tricky to sell to players. Psychologically, the end of the game signals a change of activity. The best way to overcome this is to establish the pattern from the youngest age that the session does not end with the final drill, or five a side game, but with the cool down activity which follows it. Thereby, players are taught that it is normal to finish with a cool down. It becomes second nature.

However, coaches likewise suffer from the same psychological sense that the session has already ended, and it is cool downs that are most frequently lost.

The club, school or whatever organisation providing the soccer can address this by making it a policy for all coaches to end with a cool down. The focus should be on the very youngest players here, so the lesson is established and ingrained while they are young enough to undertake it because they are told to.

Nineteen (Drill): Gentle Movement Rondo.

Aim: Warm Up while developing passing, touch and pressure skills.

Objectives:

- Keep possession by passing across a grid.
- Pass and move.
- Keep possession by passing with one or two touches.
- Close down the pass to try to intercept or force an error.

Organisation:

- 15 x 15 metre grid (This can be larger or smaller depending on the number of players. Try not to get too many involved in one grid as this will reduce movement and slow the warm up process)
- 5 v 1 players ideal. If numbers are likely to be smaller, then set up circular drill areas where 3 v 1 is feasible. It is important if using a square grid that there are at least five attackers, or gaps will appear reducing passing options.
- One attacker on each side of the grid, plus one who starts from anywhere and begins the passing movement.

- One defender inside the grid.

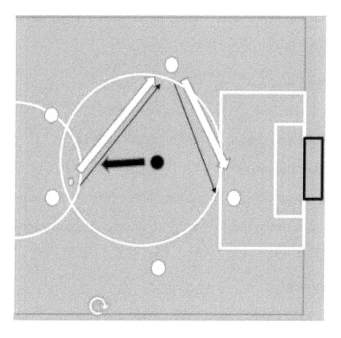

Operation of Drill:

- Play begins with a pass from one of the players who are 'doubled' on their side of the grid. (If the area is circular, then any outside player can begin.)
- That player then passes to another teammate then runs to where they have passed the ball.
- Defenders try to intercept pass, win the ball after the first touch or force a pass that goes beyond a teammate.

- When possession is lost, the pressing defender swaps positions with the attacker who has given away possession.

Key Skills:

- Players seek to be on the move at all times.
- This includes moving after the pass, moving to improve angles in order to receive a pass, or moving to pressure the pass.

Development:

- No real development for this drill, since the purpose is to keep it familiar and simple and encourage gentle activity.

Twenty (Drill): Steal and Score

Aim: Warm up while developing dribbling skills

Objectives:

- Dribble within an area.

- Attempt to score in a small goal.

- Attempt to win the ball.

Organisation:

- Small grid or circle.
- Any number of players, but there should be two more attackers than defenders.
- Ball for each attacker.
- Small goal in the centre. Cones can be used.

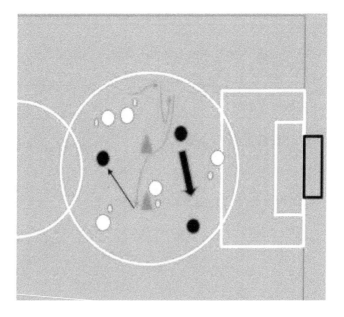

Operation of Drill:

- Players must dribble within the grid area and score a point if they can dribble the ball into or through the goal.
- When a goal is scored, they must pass to a defender, and then become the defender themselves.
- Defenders can also get a ball by tackling an opponent or picking up a loose ball.
- This warm up can become a little more competitive than the previous rondo drill, so if a spare adult can supervise with younger players this is probably wise…

Key Skills:

- Players develop close dribbling skills.
- Warm up or cool down.

Development:

- As before, no real development for this drill, since the purpose is to keep it familiar and simple and encourage gentle activity.

Twenty-One (Drill): No Flagging

Aim: Improve dribbling while warming up.

Objectives:

- Dribble between flags.

Organisation:

- The simplest of warm up drills. Place a number of flags inside a large grid. Keep them randomly placed.
- Any number v 1 players.
- Each player, other than the defender, has a ball.

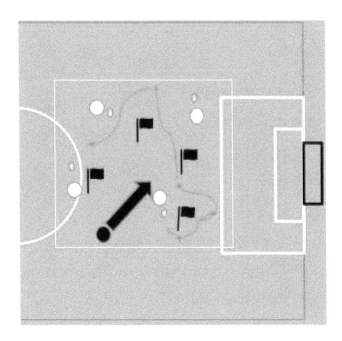

Operation of Drill:

- Simply dribble the ball around the flags.
- Defender attempts to kick a ball out of the grid.
- Player who lost ball collects it, passes it to the defender and then becomes the new defender themselves.
- Energy and enthusiasm can fall with this drill, so keep it fairly short.

Key Skills:

- Tight dribbling skills.
- Protecting the ball.

Development:

- Use different coloured flags or cones.
- Each colour represents a skill to practise as the player dribbles towards it.
- For example, there are three blue, three red and three yellow flags in the grid. Do a step over approaching a yellow flag; do a feint approaching a red flag and stand on the ball approaching a blue one.

Twenty-Two (Coaching Strategy): Starting and Ending a Session

The best coaches are well prepared. They recognise that the start and end of a session are particularly important and plan these elements as closely as the drills on which they will focus during training. Arrive a little early and set up three or four warm up drills in a corner of the field. They can be left up during the session and used to cool down at the end.

By having several drills ready, players can move through them quickly and younger players will not lose focus. This means that the coach can concentrate on other matters, such as greeting players, or going through tactical and technique points with individuals after the practice.

Clearly, there is often demand on training facilities, and it may not be possible to set up in advance, but by using a small number of drills with which the players are familiar, they can quickly be put in place by the first players to arrive at a session. Coaches of younger teams, especially, might find a band of very willing helpers…

In this chapter we have taken a brief look at the theory behind the important activities of warming up and cooling down. The key points we have aimed to make are:

- Warming up and cooling down are equally important.
- Cooling down tends to be the area which is frequently omitted from plans.
- A club should establish a policy regarding this area.
- Rondo drills make perfect warming up and cooling down activities, satisfying these primary aims whilst also using the time to develop skills and techniques.

- However, warm up and cooling down rondo drills should be simple so that they need little or no explanation and can become player led.
- Having the drills set up in advance is beneficial if practical.

Using Rondo Soccer Drills to Improve Teamwork

Little preamble is required here. The case for teamwork is not one it is necessary to make. However, it is worthwhile to remind readers that using rondo drills to develop teamwork will not only satisfy this aim but provide all the other benefits provided by these kinds of drills which was outlined earlier.

Using rondos is a win, win situation in developing our team's collaboration, support and understanding of each other.

Twenty-Three (Drill): Six v Six Plus Six (V1)

Aim: Improve teamwork by getting quickly into supportive positions.

Objectives:

- Keep possession by passing within a grid.
- Use boxed players as supports.

- Get into a position to receive the next pass.
- Defense works as a unit to pressure ball and close down passing options.

Organisation:

- Large rectangular grid. Inside grid are six coned boxes, approx. 2m x 2m. Only the 'box team' can enter these grids, and they must not leave them.
- 6 v 6 + 6 players; the drill can be adapted using a smaller grid to 4 v 4 + 4, here only the corner boxes are used.
- Two teams in the grid, with one ball. Third team are the box team, and they go one player in each small box.

Operation of Drill:

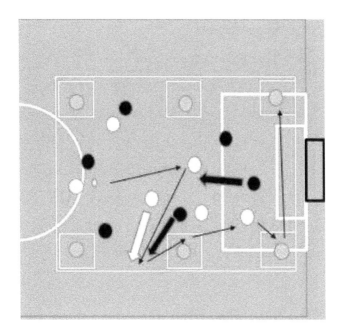

- Play begins with team in possession passing within grid. Allow up to three or four touches to begin with. With advanced players, this can become two or even one touch soccer.
- Players use players in the grid to change the angle of the pass, by passing into the box where the player cannot be tackled.
- Team in possession quickly get into position to receive the next pass.

- Box team player can pass to either the team in possession, or to another member of their own team in another box.
- Teams score a point for every three passes they can complete without involving a box player.
- Rotate teams regularly. Because there is a fair degree of failure in this drill in the early stages of its use, it is worth rotating using time, say three minutes per rotations, instead of when the ball is lost. If the ball is lost, the coach can restart the drill in a way that replays the manoeuvre which just failed.

Key Skills:

- This is a high-pressure game, because of the numbers involved, and therefore quality passing along with quality touch are needed. The coach may wish to stop the drill to run through control and passing techniques if the drill is not working.
- Moving into position quickly to receive the next pass from the box player.
- Decision making to get into a strong position to receive the following pass.

- Movement after passing to get into position for the pass after that.
- Communication with teammates.
- This drill is excellent at encouraging players to see themselves as a part of a team, and also at encouraging them to see a picture of what is developing.
- Defenders must work together to close down space as quickly as possible.
- Body position for closing down – on the half turn, pushing players towards the direction the defender wishes them to play.
- Support defense players working to the plan and picking up positions to defend or intercept subsequent passes.

Development:

- The drill does involve many players, and for younger and less experienced exponents of the game it may be necessary to reduce the number of defenders to allow the offensive units to develop the necessary skills required in the drill.

Twenty-Four (Drill): 6 v 6 + 6 V2

This drill works as the one explained in tip 23, with two significant differences which make it much harder still.

Both involve the box team. Firstly, in this version they must pass to another offensive player, rather than having the possibility of passing to a different member of the box team. Secondly, the pass must be played through a different line to the one in which the ball entered.

Twenty-Five (Drill): Old Favourite

This is one of our most popular drills, adapted here for rondo use. It involves short and long passing and is both fast paced and also involves a great deal of decision making.

Aim: Choose the time for the decisive pass.

Objectives:

- Keep possession until the best time for a decisive pass arises.

- Team work to retain possession, and to quickly gain control when the ball is played longer.
- Accurate short and long passing, and a good first touch to different types of passes.
- Team work in defense, anticipating the decisive pass, and moving to prevent it, or force it under pressure.
- Pass the ball between the two end grids to score points.

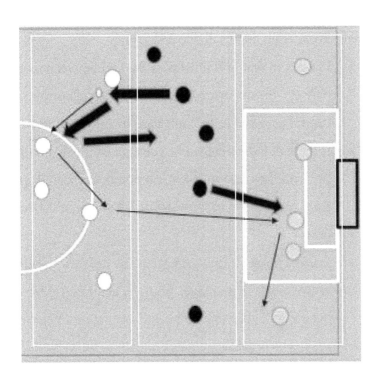

Organisation:

- 15 x 30 m grid divided into 3 lots of 10 x 15 m rectangles.
- 5 v 5 v 5 sets of players. The drill also works with groups of four or groups of six.
- The teams each fill a grid.

Operation of Drill:

- Possession begins at one end grid.
- Players in that grid must pass the ball between them until they see the opportunity for a pass through or over the central grid and to be controlled by players in the far grid.
- If the ball is intercepted or goes out of the main 30 x 15 m full grid, possession is lost, no points are scored and the team playing the pass swap with the team in the central grid.
- Players in the central grid act as the defense. They do so in two ways. One player from the central grid moves into the end grid to pressure the ball and win it or cause a bad pass. His or her teammates remain in the central grid, but drift as a unit to make an interception when the decisive pass is hit.

- When the ball reaches the other end grid, players here try to get it under control, and create the opportunity for their own decisive pass back to the opposite end.
- Meanwhile, another player from the central unit moves into the end unit to exert pressure, and the original defender returns to join his teammates in the central grid.
- Each successful decisive pass scores one point for the team making it.

Key Skills:

- Identifying the opportunity for a key pass.
- Team works to create an overlap or to switch play to create time for the pass, and space through the middle defenders to make that pass.
- Making the key pass; hit firmly through the ball, passing along the ground where possible.
- Control the long pass and lay it off quickly before pressure can be applied.
- Defending team identify the best player to pressure. Note, young players often want to 'pre plan' this, but they should not. The player to move into the end

grid will be the player best placed to apply pressure. That is a fluid situation, so cannot be pre-planned.

- Be prepared to encourage risk taking with back heels, one touch Cruyff style turns, reverse passes and passing with the outside of the foot.

Development:

- Allow a second defender into the appropriate end zone to apply more pressure there.

Twenty-Six (Drill): Variation on an Old Favourite

This drill is based on the principles of drill twenty-five but involves two teams and allows a little more thinking and control time. However, the importance of team play, of waiting for support while protecting the ball, of working together to apply pressure are still present.

Aim: Develop team work to protect the ball.

Objectives:

- One side aims to keep possession.
- The other side aim to win possession, and then retain it.

Organisation:

- Two grids of around 10 x 10 m, the actual size is not crucial. A gap of about 5 m sits between them.
- 5 v 5 players. Again, this drill will work well with anything from 3 v 3 to 6 v 6.
- Each team has its own grid. There is one ball between the two teams.

Operation of Drill:

- Two defenders move into their opponents' grid and try to win the ball.
- The team in possession attempt to retain the ball. With younger players, awarding points for successful passes, or perhaps good team support, will help to reinforce the aim of the exercise.

- When the defense wins the ball, they pass it into their own grid. If the ball leaves the grid, the attacker who lost possession must pass it into the opponents' grid.
- Players from the team who have just regained possession move back into their own grid, and two players from the team who have just lost possession, try to win it back.
- The game continues.

Key Skills:

- Players move to receive the pass. Because there are two defenders in potentially a smaller grid, this is more challenging than in the previous drill.
- Defenders work together to pressure the ball and force a mistake.
- Passing and control, especially first touch.
- Remember, a pass from the opposition team, after the ball has left their grid, may be less than sympathetic!

Development:

- Allowing extra defenders to apply pressure, reducing the size of the grid, or reducing the space between the grids all make retaining possession more challenging, heightening the importance of team work.

Twenty-Seven (Tip): Saving Time

Drills twenty-five and twenty-six are extremely complimentary of each other. A good and practical way of using them is to set up the three-zone grid in drill twenty-five, and simply use the central grid for the transition pass when possession is won by the defending side.

<u>We have looked at some drills which specifically help to develop team work in this chapter.</u> However, when we break down the components of team work, we arrive at a list which includes the following:

- Support
- Game awareness
- Communication
- Encouragement

These are attributes encouraged in all rondo drills. Thus, any rondo drill is going to be beneficial to team work. However, there is another aspect to this crucial element which rondo drills also support, but which centre around the coach her or himself.

And that is the atmosphere within the squad. The best teams have no stars. Although some players will be better than others, all are valued. All are encouraged. All have fun. That vital three letter word again. Where players have fun, they support each other. They laugh together, they pick each other up when mistakes occur, and because enjoyment supersedes winning, they actually win more often.

This is because pressure is reduced. Mistakes are seen not in a negative way, but as essential steps towards improvement. Risk taking and experimentation is encouraged, players believe in themselves, and their enjoyment increases further.

Although we are saying this again and again, it is a point that cannot be stressed often enough. Make sessions fun, whatever their focus. Rondo drills are fun, and that is why we advocate them so strongly.

Precision Passing

Why is soccer the most popular sport on the planet? There are plenty of answers to that question. Many more than we suggest below. But soccer is simple – all that is needed is a ball, or even a ball substitute. It can be played anywhere, and by anyone. It can transcend art; it can evoke the strongest of emotions. It is beautiful to watch. Goals are frequent enough to hold interest, but rare enough to be special.

ESG – When Soccer Fails to Value the Fans; the Antithesis of the Rondo

It is also tribal, and that is an important point. As such, it appeals to the most instinctive elements of mankind. We want to belong. At the time of writing this book soccer, Europe faced perhaps its biggest threat ever. Or, for the very small minority of followers who supported the proposals, it's greatest opportunity. For them. Who cares about anybody else? The European Super League, or ESL for short. Again, we are very conscious that while this is true at the time of writing, it might not be so at the time of reading. But the proposal was defeated. The tribal emotions of fans rebelled against the proposal. Their voice was made public by ex-professionals, current players and the media, and sensing a chance for some easy popularity, politicians got on the bandwagon as well. Outrage was expressed, new laws threatened, the metaphorical warships would be sent in. Much bluster and, fortunately for those politicians, no need for action. The club owners and presidents behind the scheme appear to have realised their mistake, and within forty-eight hours of proposals becoming public, like crossbars made of tape and bowler hats for gentlemen players, they were littering the soccer scrap heap.

The ESL does link to the tribal nature of soccer, and more importantly for this chapter, to the vital role of passing in the game. Since it is topical, and the cynics amongst us cannot help but feel that it will re-emerge in another form before very long, it is worth looking in a little more detail in the proposals behind the ESL.

Real Madrid is perhaps the most famous soccer club in the world. Barcelona, Manchester United and perhaps a couple of others might challenge that assertion, but most will agree that the Spanish giants, with their astonishing heritage and historical successes carry their name further into the consciousness of neutrals than any other side. But maintaining such an elevated position comes at a cost, and Real Madrid are facing financial crisis. One apparently running into billions of Euros.

The answer, it appears from the outside, was TV money. And where is that most centred? On the games between the biggest clubs.

So, logically, if more and more of those games could be organised, so the money would flow in.

The plan, which appears to have originated from the Spanish giants, but maybe did not, is that the biggest fifteen clubs in Europe will become permanent members of this league. They will be joined by five others, who could come and go. Nobody is sure how these teams will be 'invited' in; but there is reasonable belief that the likes of Leicester City, Ludogorets or Malmo would be given a chance, however successful they become in their own respective leagues,

Twelve of the original fifteen express their unbridled support for the proposition. Six are from England, who have the world's richest league (although, if the ESL goes ahead, not for much longer). These are the two Manchester Clubs, United and City; three from London – Arsenal, Chelsea and Tottenham. The most successful British team in terms of Europe, Liverpool, make up these six. Barcelona and Atletico Madrid join Real from Spain. Juventus and the two Milan clubs – Inter and AC sign up from Italy.

European Super League? There are far more than three countries on the continent. What about Germany? Bayern Munich and Dortmund are touted, but the ownership structure of clubs is different in Germany. Fans have a say, rather than exist to be exploited through overpriced tickets and burgers. They stay in the shadows. So do Paris

St Germain from France. This team is so rich compared to its domestic opponents that the only shock is that they do not always win every trophy. Still, they do not sign up.

These are the other three members, everybody assumes. Talk centres around other famous clubs, such as Celtic, or Benfica. Ajax – birthplace of the rondo – surely should be included? Perhaps they do not want to be.

These twelve are among the richest clubs but are not all the most successful. Tottenham Hotspurs, for example, have not won a major trophy for thirteen years, and that was the smallest of the domestic prizes. They have not won their league in the living memory of all but their oldest supporters. That, though, seems a small point. This prospective league is about money, not merit.

What the owners failed to grasp was the tribal factor among fans. Chelsea supporters would much rather see their team, live and in the flesh, against Derby County one season, Norwich City the next and then West Bromwich Albion, than season upon season against Real Madrid. Yes, a cup draw against one of Europe's top teams is a thrill. But it is a thrill because of its rarity. Familiarity breeds contempt. Never has the cliché been more true. Further, there is cost. Getting on a train or supporters' coach from London to Newcastle is expensive, but not bank-breakingly so. Flying out to some European capital every couple of weeks certainly is. Not only for the cost of tickets, of transport but also for the time that will need to be taken off of work. A thousand-mile round trip? OK for the occasional treat but not for a week in, week out league. Not everybody is as wealthy as the owner of a soccer club. Not everybody is prepared to take on as much debt as a Real Madrid or Barcelona. Some people prefer to live within their means.

Another element of the tribal side of supporters which those owners failed to understand is the sense of achievement that comes from avoiding relegation, the pleasurable uncertainty of risk. This is very much a cultural thing, perhaps not properly appreciated among other cultures, such as the US, where the concepts of promotion and relegation are rarely encountered in major sport. In some other cultures, the game is just one part of the entire entertainment package, in Europe, and the UK in particular, it is the package. There is nothing else. Therefore, if nothing rests on the game, then a lot of its interest goes. Under the ESL model, for half of clubs there will be little interest beyond Christmas of the traditional season. Qualification for the knock out stages is out of the question; relegation does not happen. The stresses of the ESL will mean that winning the domestic Championship is less of a reward, because every season a bigger tournament awaits. Equally, there is no need to battle for qualification for this league, since a place is guaranteed. It is unlikely that these teams will be competitive in domestic cup competitions. They will need to operate effectively two teams. That is already starting to happen in the Premier League at least, much to the derision and disgust of fans.

So, the concept was doomed in the fans' eyes. Such displeasure is often ignored, this time it was too extreme, it seems, to turn a blind eye.

But what does this have to do with passing? Quite a lot, actually. For two reasons. Firstly, in terms of the game itself scoring goals is the biggest attraction. This achievement will overwhelmingly start from a pass. The only exception is a goal scored direct from a set play. Secondly, we head back to that tribal element of soccer. The tribe's success is built on survival and conquest. A pass is the equivalent of the blow of a knife or the strike of a spear. Delivered properly it causes damage, at its best it is fatal. That is why we applaud and cheer a perfect pass, both ones which split the defence or involve a piece of insight or skill which is unexpected.

Get passing right and we not only win the game, but we gain enormous satisfaction, both as a player or coach and, in the professional game, as a fan.

Twenty-Eight (Drill): Third Line Passing

Aim: To make a decisive pass.

Objectives:

- Pass to create a goal scoring situation.
- Move to the third line, or decisive pass, as quickly as possible.
- Move to create support.
- Attempt to score.

Organisation:

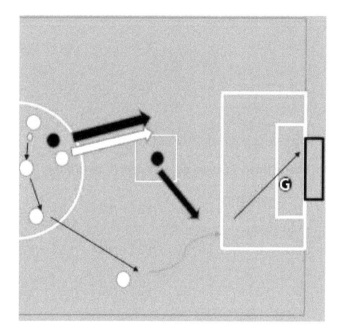

- A little more complex set up than normal here. Half a six a side pitch, is used. A second 'box' is created 10m towards the goal. A goal is needed for this drill.
- 5 v 2 plus one goalkeeper players
- 4 v 1 in the centre circle. Second defender in the box identified above. Final attacker anywhere 'onside' on the pitch.
- Goalkeeper in goal.

Operation of Drill:

- Play begins on the half way spot.
- Players must create the space for a decisive pass. They do so with quick, accurate passing to take the immediate defender out of the game.
- As the decisive pass is played, the box defender comes into play, as does the spare attacker.
- All players may now support the attack or add to the defense.
- The spare attacker attempts to score.

Key Skills:

- Understand the development of the move to create the space for the decisive pass. (Note: where this fails, the coach should point out what went wrong, if the players themselves are unable to do so.)
- Judge the point and position to play the third line, or decisive, pass.
- Have the skills to play the decisive pass. Ideally, along the ground, into space for the striker to run on to, but in a way that takes the box defender out of the game.

- Shooting skills.
- Developing covering defense to slow the crucial pass. For example, pressuring on the half turn, so the defender can quickly move to pressure the next receiver. Not diving in to win the ball unless there has been a mis-control. Looking for the misplaced pass which might offer the opportunity to take possession.

Development:

- Limit the number of passes that can be made before the third line, decisive pass.

Twenty-Nine (Drill): Third Line Pass Under Increasing Pressure

As we have tried to achieve in the previous drill, making the decisive pass must be reasonably quick. With each short pass, the defense has more time to become organised, particularly is the passing is lateral or backwards.

This is the same drill, but with more players. Now two teams of six. The extra striker is involved in the first stage. The extra defenders are based outside of the centre circle (or grid). The first pass is free, but at each subsequent pass an extra defender can enter the centre circle and attempt to win the ball. Thus, making the decisive pass becomes harder, and this encourages the offensive team to find the opportunity as quickly as possible.

Thirty (Tactic): Timing the Run

A rondo is at its most effective when it leads to a clear goal scoring opportunity. This is most often achieved when a player makes a well-timed run. This involves a good understanding of the development of play, and of one's teammates. Look for the point at which a player in possession has time and space, and then make the run, calling for the ball. At an advanced level, make the run which favours the likely direction of pass. Avoid a run which forces a player to pass through heavy traffic, or lift the ball, which is much harder to control on receipt.

Thirty-One (Coaching Strategy): Use the Experience of the Best when Making Runs

Coaches should encourage their players to study professionals through video clips and post-match TV analysis to understand how and why players make runs, and how these assist the making of the decisive pass.

Thirty-Two (Drill): Rondo drill to Create Space for A Decisive Run

Aim: Create the space for a decisive pass for runners.

Objectives:

- Use the rondo to keep possession AND create time for a decisive, third line, pass.
- Pass and move to support the striker.
- Striker develops understanding of when to make their run.
- Striker learns to be prepared to make multiple runs.

Organisation:

- 15 x 15 metre grid near half way line.
- Mannequin to represent defender. A real defender can be used once the players become adept at the drill. Goal.
- 6 v 2 plus a keeper

- One striker is ready to make a run. He begins wide of the grid and in front of it. The other offensive players use the grid. Four around the outside, one in the grid.
- Two defenders attempt to slow down the delivery of the decisive pass by closing space.
- They try to judge when the opportunity arises to win the ball.

Operation of Drill:

- Play begins with a backwards pass from the attacking player in the grid.
- Players in the rondo seek to pass quickly to create an overload on one side, or space through the middle for the decisive pass.
- Defenders try to intercept pass, win the ball after the first touch or force a pass that goes beyond a teammate.
- When the offensive team has space, and the striker making the run is in a good position, they play the decisive, third line, pass.
- Striker runs on and attempts to score. Mannequin or real defender attempts to prevent the attempt.
- Striker making the run: this player should always be moving. They seek to anticipate the pass which will lead to the space for the decisive pass. When the pass happens, they accelerate laterally across the pitch, straightening up as a teammate receives a pass in space. They then straighten towards goal and run onto the third line, decisive, pass.

Key Skills:

- Passing progressively to make the space for the decisive pass.
- Be aware of teammates, both the one making the final run, and other teammates in the grid.
- Defenders anticipate offensive moves to slow down the delivery of the decisive pass.
- Timing runs.
- Precision passing.
- Finishing.

Development:

- Use a real defender instead of a mannequin.
- Introduce a second run maker, and a second defender to stop this.

Thirty-Three (Tactic): Runners from Midfield

With defences ever more efficient, right from junior levels upwards, often the best way to break down such organisation is through runners from midfield. The secret is timing, to come from deep so it is harder for the defense to pick up. Encourage all players to try making runs from deep, assuring them that even if they do not get the ball themselves, they will be creating space for teammates.

Thirty-Four (Drill): Rondo Leading to Pass to Runner from Midfield Number 1

Aim: Create the space to get the ball to a runner from midfield.

Objectives:

- Create the space to feed the ball into a deep lying striker.
- Time runs past this striker.
- Get in an attempt at goal.
- Aim to prevent the key pass or slow it down.

Organisation:

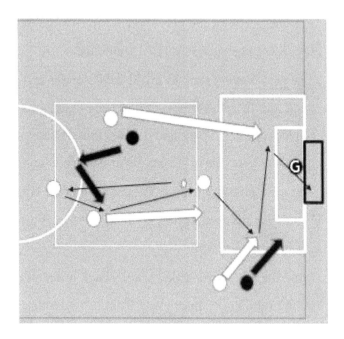

- 10 x 10 m grid 10 m in front of the penalty area.
- 5 v 2 (4 v 1 + 1 + 1) players plus a keeper
- Three attackers and one defender are inside the grid, or on the outside. A further attacker waits on the edge of the grid nearest the goal.
- The offense seeks to pass quickly to create the space for this attacker to turn and feed in a pass to the lone striker.
- The lone striker is marked by the other defender, who must remain goal side for the drill.

Operation of Drill:

- Play begins with the player on the front edge of the grid laying a pass backwards to a teammate.
- The grid players seek to avoid the defender and get a pass back into this player giving him time to turn. (Note: if this player receives a pass and decides that he cannot turn and get away a key pass, he can lay it back to a teammate.)
- The grid defender tries to intercept a pass or win the ball.
- When the advanced grid play turns to lay off the pass, three things happen.
- First, the advanced striker comes back to receive the ball, giving him some space away from his defender, who must remain goal side.
- Secondly, the two widest players from grid break fast to try to get in an advance position from midfield.
- Thirdly, the passer advances after making his or her pass to their striker.
- The striker looks to lay the ball off to one of the players breaking from midfield.
- These players look to score.

Key Skills:

- Fast, tight short passing to create space.
- Judging the time to turn and pass.
- Turning quickly and passing accurately on the turn, along the ground.
- Playing a lay off.
- Breaking fast from midfield.
- Shooting.

Development:

- As players become more adept at making the runs, allow the final defender to become less passive.

We have deviated slightly from the main objective of this chapter, which is developing rondos to provide precise passing, although the drill above does enhance this skill. Let us return to a more traditional rondo, where we seek to help players play passes through the defense, sometimes called second line passing.

In order to do this, we need to employ effective first line passing, which is passing around the defense to create the time and space for a decisive pass. Such a pass is the one which breaks a well organised defense. It will not create a goal scoring opportunity immediately but will lead to the opportunity of advancing an attack.

Thirty-Five (Drill): Precise Passing through the line

Aim: Create the space for a pass through the defensive line.

Objectives:

- Use fast, lateral, passing to split the defense.
- Pass through the defense.

Organisation:

- 10 x 5 metre grid. (This can be larger or smaller depending on the skill level of the players.)
- 6 v 2 players.
- Two attackers along each long side of the grid, one on each short side.

Operation of Drill:

- Play begins with one player passing to any of their teammates. After that initial pass, the drill begins.

- Players seek to pass the ball quickly to create the opportunity for a pass across the grid from one long side to the other.

- Defenders try to prevent this key pass through them. They must judge the extent to which they are drawn out from the centre of the grid.

- A point is scored for every successful across the grid and through the defense. This is awarded to all offensive players. If the group is very competitive, scores can be compared at the end.

- When possession is lost, the pressing defender swaps positions with the attacker who has given away possession. Both defenders score a point.

Key Skills:

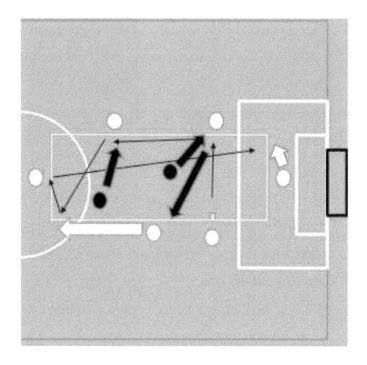

- Fast passing to split defense and create the gap to pass through them.
- Defense with a picture of the developing game, to present the point scoring cross grid pass.

Development:

- Turn the grid into a 10 x 10 m square, with four attackers and two defenders.

Thirty-Six: (Coaching Strategy)

The next four drills each practise a different kind of pass. However, the different types of passing can be used in any of the drills. In practical terms, we suggest setting up one of the drills, then using it to practise all passing types. Then next week, a different basic drill can be set up, again to work on a variety of passing styles. This helps to keep the drills fresh for players.

Thirty-Seven (Drill): Precision passing using instep – creating triangles

Aim: To keep possession using triangles.

Objectives:

- One or two touch passes.
- Move to create triangles, to ensure there is always a passing option.
- Pass correctly – see key skills.

Organisation:

- Very simple. A small grid can be used to set parameters, but with experienced players this is not necessary, simply explain that aim is to remain no more than 5 metres apart.
- 3 v 1 players

Operation of Drill:

- Pass using the instep, and one or two touches, to keep possession.
- If defender wins possession, he or she swaps with the player who lost possession.

Key Skills:

- Players constantly on the move, to ensure there are always two passing options, meaning the defender can only close out one.
- Good touch and body position to allow rapid passing.
- Passing technique:
- Position so planted foot ends up approx. 30cm or one foot from the kicking foot.
- Point the planted foot towards the direction of the pass to be made.
- Keep the passing foot horizontal to the ground.
- Use some back lift, the more the back lift the firmer the pass.
- Stay loose and relaxed.

- Strike smoothly through the ball, with hips facing the direction of pass.
- Lean slightly forwards and sideways to keep the ball on the floor and to ensure accuracy.

Thirty-Eight (Drill): Precision Passing using the outside of the foot – the 'give and go'

Aim: Pass accurately with the outside of the foot. Create space for the 'give and go.'

(Note: 'Give and go' is a soccer specific term, adapted for some other sports, where the passer immediately sprints after giving the pass to a new position, encouraging the receiver to play a return pass.

Objectives: These are largely the same as in the previous drill.

- Keep possession by passing across a grid.
- Receive the ball in the correct body position to make the next pass.
- Keep possession by passing with one or two touches.
- Move to support a teammate, creating a 'give and go' scenario.

Organisation:

- Circular area, approximately 10 m in diameter
- 4 v 1 players
- Pass and move, ending up in a position to receive a return pass.

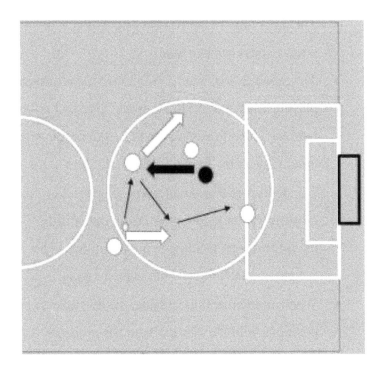

Operation of Drill:

- Play begins with one player passing to any of their teammates.
- The passer moves across the grid to a new position where a return pass can be made.
- The receiver does not have to make the return pass to the player; in the match situation the 'give and go' is used both to run on to a return pass, and to create space for other players by drawing a defender.
- The defenders tries to intercept the pass. For this drill, they must remain at least a metre from the outside of the playing area, so tackling is not permitted. This is because the passing technique is more challenging.
- When an interception is made, the defender swaps positions with the attacker who has given away possession.

Key Skills:

- Key skills of the outside of the foot pass:
- Receive the ball on the half turn to protect the ball.

- Control the ball slightly in front of the body if using two touches.
- Control the ball approximately 6 inches / 15 cm in front of the body.
- Plant the non-kicking foot just under one foot / 30 cm away from the ball and pointing about 45 degrees short of the intended direction of pass.
- Pass using the same motion as when passing with the instep, back-lift, body lean forwards and slightly to the side, arms for balance, strike firmly on the ball, but using the outside of the foot just in front of the laces. Follow through.
- Remember, the ball will curve away with the rotation placed on it, so aim slightly to your left of the receiver if right footed, slightly to the right if left footed.
- There is a second outside of the foot pass for very short passes. Here, push rather than strike the ball.
- Push the ball with the foot slightly lifted, to keep it on the ground.
- This is a pass to use for a short, and largely lateral pass.
- Moving for the 'give and go':
- As the pass is made, sprint hard to a new position, giving an angle for the return pass.

- Shout 'Yes' or 'Back' while sprinting. As a team, try to develop a consistent call to avoid confusion.
- On reaching the receiving point (the edge of the circle in this drill).

Thirty-Nine (Drill): Precision Passing Using Weaker Foot – Two Pass Switching Play

Aims: Improve passing with the weaker foot. Ideally, to the extent that it becomes no longer the weaker foot.

Objectives:

- Switch the direction of play to stretch a defense.
- Receive the ball in the correct body position – on the half turn - to make the next pass.
- Create space for a shot.
- Move to score rebounds.

Organisation:

- Width of the penalty area.
- 3 v 1 players plus a keeper. (Multiple teams can be set up,)

- Plenty of balls.

- Attack players on the corners of the box. One in the D.

- Defensive player starts between players one and two.

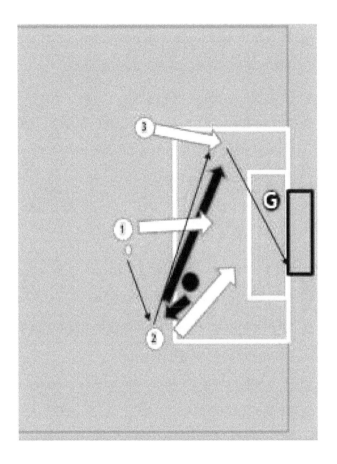

Operation of Drill:

- Player one passes to player two.
- Player two across with one or two touches to player three.
- Player three shoots with one or two touches.
- Other attackers move in for rebounds.
- Defensive player attempts to get across and close down player three. However, to make the drill realistic to the match situation, they must move towards each player when they are in possession.

Key Skills:

- The key player here is player two.
- Depending on time, they have two ways in which to complete the switch of play.
- The point their shoulder towards the passer, putting them on the half turn.
- If the defender is closing quickly, they either sweep the ball on with the instep, first time, or turn their outside foot towards the ball, and control with the outside of the foot. This will take the ball across their body and away from the

defender. They then pass with the same foot completing the switch.

- Another method is to feint to take the ball in front of the body, but let it roll across to the far foot. They then turn and pass it on first time.

- Be prepared to encourage risk taking with passes in this situation. Back heels, flicks and running towards the ball and passing first time with the inside or outside of the foot are all reasonable, if difficult, alternative ways of switching play quickly.

- Player three shoots across the keeper and back towards the far post.

Forty (Drill): Precision Passing Including a 180-degree turn

Aim: Turning at speed.

Objectives:

- Keep possession with accurate passing and using turns.

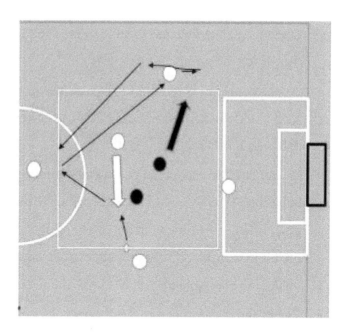

Organisation:

- 15 x 15 metre grid.
- 5 v 2 players.
- One attacker on each side of the grid, one in the middle. Extra attacker starts with the drill with a pass to any teammate. Two defenders in the grid. Players inside the grid cannot leave it.

Operation of Drill:

- Play begins with one player passing to any of their teammates.
- The passer runs to where they have passed.
- Defenders try win the ball.
- When possession is lost, the pressing defender swaps positions with the attacker who has given away possession.
- At least every third pass, the receiver must change the direction of the ball with a 180 degree turn prior to the next pass.

Key Skills:

- For the turn:
- Control the ball laterally to about one foot / 30 cm from the body.
- Complete a turn. This can be any kind of turn. Some coaching points for turning are included below.
- Pass the ball in the change of direction.
- Coach keeps it light and fun.

Two Turns to Use:

Cruyff Turn:

- o *Plant the opposite foot firmly.*
- o *Raise opposite arm for balance and disguise.*
- o *Opponent should commit to blocking the pass, placing them off balance.*
- o *As the foot approaches the ball for the fake pass, rotate it so that it points at the other foot.*
- o *Drag the ball back 180 degrees, dropping and rotating at the same time.*

Hook Turn:

- o *Passer places outside foot between defender and ball.*
- o *Passer hooks the ball back 180 degrees using the outside of the foot.*
- o *Passer moves play on by passing away from the defender.*

The hook turn can be played using both an inside and an outside hook. Each can be seen here:

Inside Hook: How to Do an Inside Hook | Soccer Skills - YouTube

Inside Hook Link: https://www.youtube.com/watch?v=h_b7ObXN9Oo

Outside Hook: How to Do an Outside Hook | Soccer Skills - YouTube

Outside Hook Link: https://www.youtube.com/watch?v=vKI_DphaToo

Cruyff Turn: How to do the Maradona & Cruyff Turn - Football Soccer Move Tutorial - YouTube

Cruyff Turn Link: https://www.youtube.com/watch?v=zVEeum8wA6U

Reverse Pass: Here are some examples of the reverse, or disguised, pass, executed by perhaps its greatest exponent of the last decade, the mercurial Mesut Ozil.

Mesut Özil Signature Pass - The Disguised Pass - YouTube

Reverse Pass Link:

https://www.youtube.com/watch?v=1QVsDM6aow8

Forty-One (Drill): Indoor Passing – the Sole of the Game!

This drill works best on a hard surface, such as an artificial pitch, an indoor facility or tarmac. However, it is a skill which will transfer to the full sided game as well.

Aim: Use the sole of the foot as an additional tool to keep possession.

Objectives:

- Keep possession by short passing in a tight area.
- Control the pass in a way that allows possession to be retained.

Organisation:

- Small playing area. It is not necessary to mark out a grid here because there is little movement from the attacking players.
- 5 v 1 players.
- Move the ball rapidly to keep possession, using the sole at least once in each manoeuvre.

Operation of Drill:

- Play begins with one player passing to another.
- The receiver must use the sole of their foot in at least one of the moves they make in passing the ball on.
- They can stop the ball dead by stepping on it. Here they focus on keeping arms out for balance, and the non-kicking foot planted firmly for stability.
- They can control the ball with the inside or outside of their foot, they pass it on by either rolling it forwards with the sole of the foot, or (more commonly) dragging it back to pass it with the sole. This kind of pass benefits from disguise to wrong foot the defender.
- They can control the ball, then use the sole to roll it backwards and forwards to dummy the defender before passing.
- They can stand on the ball, drag it back and rotate to change direction.
- As usual, when the ball is lost, passer and defender swap positions.

Key Skills:

- Players move quickly and confidence.
- They seek to disguise their intentions using body movements, movement of the ball or eye and head movements.
- Coach keeps the session light and fun and encourages experimentation.

Forty-Two (Drill): One and Two Touch Passing

Aim: Develop touch while keeping concentration.

Objectives:

- Keep possession by passing across a grid.
- Keep concentrating on the game.

Organisation:

- 10 x 10 metre.

- 4 v 1 players. More players can be included, and the grid enlarged.
- Alternate one and two touch passing.

Operation of Drill:

- Standard possession-based rondo, passing across and around the grid to retain the ball.
- Standard role of the defender, and usual swapping methods after an error.
- The challenge comes from the requirement to alternate one and two touch passing. Players must therefore concentrate on every pass, so that they know how many touches to use when they receive a pass.

Key Skills:

- Concentration.
- Communication.

Key Conclusions from this Chapter

The point we have sought to make is that rondo drills can be used to help develop all kinds of passing activities, and all styles of passing. This can be the primary aim of the drill, or a secondary benefit of it.

Breaking Down the Defense, the Line Splitting Pass

Now it is time to build upon the varieties of precision passing presented in the previous chapter. In this chapter we will look at drills specifically designed to break lines – this includes playing out from the back, playing through midfield, the long switch, feeding the ball through defensive lines between the opponents' midfield and defense and finally the assist – the pass that leads to, hopefully, a goal.

Forty-Three (Tactic): Playing Out from the Back

We will look in much more details at dealing with the high press in a later chapter. However, the goalkeeper is often the crucial player when it comes to playing out from the back. In the past, keepers might have undertaken their own training. While there is definitely some position specific work keepers should undertake, we advise including them in all rondo drills.

Forty-Four (Coaching Strategy): Meet Our New Number 10 – Formerly the Centre Half

Without wishing to push the point, the same argument applies to defensive players, especially centre halves. It is worth watching some top-level games where one side applies the high press and the other plays out from the back.

Note how the pressing team try to isolate the least talented passing centre back. Or the keeper. The primary aim of the high press is to win possession high up the park, but that is not always possible. The secondary aim then becomes to leave the final pass out to this relatively weak player of the ball. Then, the chance of a damaging pass being played forward is reduced. The centre half, or keeper, left to make this pass will often just look to clear the ball, hitting it long and high. That gives the pressing team a high probability of winning the ball and being able to launch forwards again.

It is clear, and reasonable, that coaches might want to use more creative players as the offense in rondo drills, and let defensive units work together in the underloaded teams. While it makes sense to let the defense work together we would argue that in a rondo drill their focus must be more on developing their own positive skills, rather than always defensive ones.

Forty-Five (Tactic): Keep It on the Deck

The most successful teams often win in one of two ways. Either they dominate possession and win through the weight of chances. Or they absorb pressure but break with devastating effect. In either case, every player must have a good first touch, see patterns of play and develop a picture of the development of their team's game, and have the skills to deliver quality passing.

This is most easily achieved playing the ball along the floor. We advocate the tactic of pass and move, with short, accurate passing, reducing the opportunity for loss of possession. Clearly, rondo drills assist with this tactic, but even without the rondo it remains the future of the game.

Enough theorising, let us get on with some more rondo drills!

Forty-Six (Drill): When it goes wrong…

As wonderful playing out from the back might look, and as effective as it is, good teams and coaches recognise that it does not always work, and there must be a plan B. The following drill seeks to create the space for the long pass out from the back, and then works on how to utilise that long pass to retain possession.

Aim: Play the long pass with safety and accuracy in mind.

Objectives:

- Create the space and time for a long pass.
- Play the long pass accurately.
- Bring the long pass into an attacking situation.

Organisation:

- This is a fairly complicated drill, which needs some setting up and explanation.
- 8 v 4 players.
- Two 15 x 10 m grids approximately 20 m apart, depending on the age of the players. The player making the long pass

133

will need to kick the ball from the back of their grid to wide of the opposite grid, so distance may need to be reduced for younger players.

- Cones 5 m back from the playing grids form a rectangle.
- Grid with ball contains three attackers and two defenders. A fourth attacker waits in the zone behind the grid but inside the cones. This is the player who will make the long pass.
- The opposite large grid contains the other two defenders. The remaining attackers split 2 and 2 outside the opposite grid, but inside the cones.

Operation of Drill:

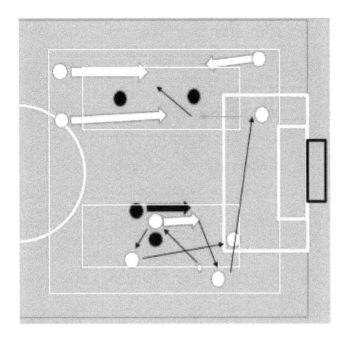

- Play starts with the long passer, who plays a short pass into the grid.
- Players pass to create the space for an accurate forward ball to their teammates further up field.
- If they cannot create the space to do so by the fourth pass, they must pass back to the long passer. The defense cannot leave the grid to tackle this player.
- The long passer hits a high, angled pass trying to find their teammates further up the pitch.

135

- Once this pass is played, the attackers recently in possession set up 2 and 2 as their teammates have been. They are ready to receive the long pass from the other direction.
- The up field attackers will either have received the ball with an accurate, along the ground pass, or a challenging high pass.
- In either case, they bring the ball under control, and bring it into the grid with a dribble or pass.
- The other two attackers who did not receive the long pass, join them.
- One player moves behind the grid to become the next long passer.
- Once the ball is in the grid, the ball is played back to the new long passer, who plays it back to a teammate in the grid and the drill continues as before.

Key Skills:

- Playing the long pass.
- Long touch the ball approximately one to two metres in front. Remember, the defense is not allowed out of the grid, so they cannot make a tackle.

- Approach the ball at an angle and plant the non-kicking foot approximately one foot / 30 cm beside and in line with the rear of the ball.
- Bend the planted leg at the knee.
- Point the hips and the planted foot in the direction of the pass.
- Strike the ball firmly, hitting low down and leaning slightly backwards to get elevation and sideways to retain accuracy.
- Strong follow through.
- Teammates anticipate movement of defense to give options for the pass.
- Defense works as a unit to restrict passing options and create pressure.

Development:

- Remove the outer cones to force the last defender / keeper to play the ball under pressure.

Forty-Seven (Drill): Passing Through the Lines

Aim: Pass the ball through multiple grids to create a scoring opportunity.

Objectives:

- Keep possession until the opportunity arises for a key, through the line pass.
- Receive the ball in the correct body position to make the next pass.
- Be aware of action in the other grids.
- Advance and retreat in line with the action.

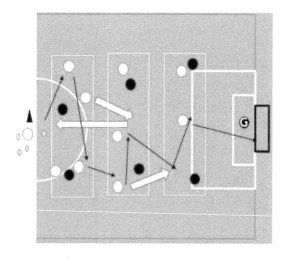

138

- Three 10 x 5 m grids, with a 5 m gap between them.
- Cone for starting player.
- Goal 10m back from final grid.
- Feeder starts by cone, with balls.
- First 'defensive third' grid 4 v 2. (For weaker players, this can be 4 v 1 to make it harder for the defense to disrupt.)
- Second 'middle third' grid 3 v 2, moving to 4 v 2.
- 'Final third' grid 2 v 2, moving to 3 v 2.

Operation of Drill:

- Play begins with the feeder who passes the ball into the defensive third grid.
- Using rondo play movement, the players in this grid make the room for a pass into the middle grid.
- One attacking player from the defensive third runs into the middle grid to support.
- Passing creates space for a pass into the final third. Again, a player from the middle third can advance into this third to support.
- Players attempt to create space for a shot on goal.

- Once the ball has left a particular grid, the player who has advanced into it MUST retreat to their original grid. This rule is important, especially in the variations which follow in the next two drills.
- If the drill breaks down at any stage, or the coach feels progress is too slow, then play begins again from the feeder, and all players return to their original grid.
- Swap positions every couple of minutes.

Key Skills:

- There are two particular skills which we have not directly practised before.
- Players must protect the ball while they wait for support to complete the overload.
- Receive the ball on the half turn, use the body to protect it, lay the ball off or turn.
- Communication.
- The second skill particular to this drill is moving quickly to support the players further up the pitch. If support does not arrive quickly then the defense will become too organised to break down quickly.

Development:

- Try the drill removing the grids, with the feeder becoming the equivalent of a last defender or goalkeeper.
- While the grids help to contain the play, and encourage passing, the open pitch is more realistic to the match situation.

Forty-Eight (Drill): Through the Lines, complex version

This drill follows the basic pattern of drill forty-seven. However, play is speeded up.

This time, the feeder can play a ball into the defensive third as soon as he or she wishes, provided they stick to the over-riding rule that there can be only one ball in each grid at any moment.

This means that players in the grid must keep possession until the next grid on has cleared their ball. Potentially, three balls should be in play at any one moment.

This added complexity focusses concentration and encouraged players to adapt to their circumstances.

Forty-Nine (Drill): Ultimate Playing Through the Lines

Once more, the basic drill is the same, but we add another twist now, which allows the ball to be played backwards when a forward pass proves unachievable.

The one ball in a grid rule applies, so if, for example, there is a ball in every grid, when the final third ball is passed back to the middle third, so their ball must be played back to the defensive third, and in turn their ball is returned to the feeder.

To help keep some order to the drill, and to add a target, give the feeder ten balls. Allow five minutes for the drill. Any ball returned to the feeder can be used again. But if there are ever two balls in a grid, both are lost (the coach might need to be a bit flexible here, depending on the age and level of the players). Balls are also lost if any defender is able to kick them out of the grid, or a pass between grids does not reach its destination.

Award five points for every goal scored in the five minutes, three points for every shot on target and one point for every shot from the final third which misses the target. Par is 18 points. There's a target to beat…

Fifty (Drill): Rondo drills for crossing

Aim: Create the space for a cross.

Objectives:

- Use one and two touch passing to create space for a cross.
- Attempt to cross into a danger area.

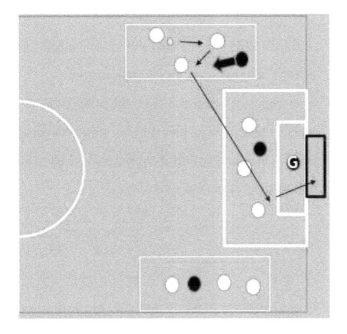

Organisation:

- 2 timnes10 x 5 m grid on either side of the pitch.
- Penalty area as third grid.
- Goal.
- 3 x 1 players in each wide grid. 3 x 1 players in the penalty area plus a keeper.

Operation of Drill:

- A simple drill. Create space to cross the ball into the penalty area to create an attempt on goal.
- Then repeat the exercise from the other side.
- Rotate the groups of four players both between grids / penalty area and within the groups so all have the opportunity to play as defender.

Key Skills:

- Create space by drawing defender towards one side of the grid.
- Either pass to an overlapping player for an out swinging cross or pull back for an inswinger.

- Crossing the ball:
- ➢ Either knock the ball half a metre away from the kicking foot, or striker the ball first time.
- ➢ In either case, plant the non-kicking foot beside the ball, approximately 10 inches / 24 cm from the ball.
- ➢ Position the hips at an angle to the ball.
- ➢ Strike the ball firmly with the instep, leaning slightly backwards.
- ➢ Use the arms for balance and strike through the ball.

Development:

- Crosses do not have to be high for headers, play the ball in along the ground.
- Aim to get to the by-line and pull the ball away from the keeper.

Fifty-One (Drill): Match related Crossing

Aim: Create space for an overlap.

Objectives:

- Commit a defender to allow an overlapping player to get wide and cross the ball.

Organisation:

- 5 x 5 m grid.
- 2 v 1 players plus a receiver if required.

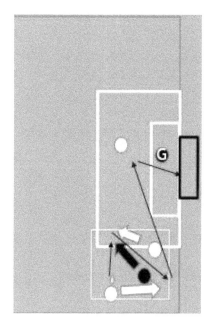

Operation of Drill:

- Within the grid, draw the defender to one corner.

- Partner without the ball accelerates outside of the player in possession and out of the grid.
- Pass is played through.
- Cross.
- Next set of players go.

Key Skills:

- Short passing to create the space for the overlap.
- Crossing the ball as per the technique outlined above.

Development:

- Enlarge the drill into a 5 v 3 half pitch game.

Fifty-Two (Tactic): Where to Place a Cross

We are talking here about age groups where heading is permitted, as well as the adult game. However, statistics for lower crosses for shots are not vastly different. Indeed, in some circumstances, for example, when the defense is stretched, a low cross into a player running in can be amazingly effective.

However, when crossing for a header, the results are not too surprising. The most effective cross is from level with the penalty area, about mid-way between the corner of the area and the by-line. Any cross which can be headed between the posts is more effective than a deep or short cross. Slightly shorter crosses, that is ones that are headed inside the posts but before the penalty spot, are most effective of all.

Fifty-Three (Coaching Strategy): Does the Cross have a Part to Play in Modern Soccer?

Traditionalists will be pleased to hear that statistically the answer is 'yes'. Purists will be equally pleased to hear that this part is pretty small – much smaller than would be guessed from the play of many professional teams…but not the most successful ones.

The whole concept of crossing as a team coaching strategy came under scrutiny after Liverpool attempted to build their attacking play around it in 2011. They bought the giant striker Andy Carroll and filled the team with the best crossers they could find. During the season, they delivered 787 crosses in their 38 Premier League matches (trust me, I didn't count them – some people clearly have too much time on their hands) and this led to wait for it. Four goals.

However, further analysis suggested that this appalling rate of return was because Liverpool were both too predictable in their playing style and crossed from too deep. So keen were they to get the ball into the box that they crossed far too soon, and that made defending easy.

Statistics suggest that it takes, on average, 92 crosses to score a goal. But, as we know, statistics are fond of lying. Actually, when second phases such as knock downs, rebounds, corners and penalties are taken into account, the figure improves to one in 45. It is when we look at crosses delivered to the best spot from the best position that analysis shows a success rate of about one in 14. A far more palatable figure. Although, of course, even this data is not being strictly honest. If a team aimed to play every cross from the same optimum position and land it on the same optimum point, defences would adapt, and cut out both the supply and the end result. It is the very fact that many crosses do not land in the best spot that means that when they do, there is a higher chance of a goal being scored.

Fifty-Four (Drill): The Reverse Pass

There is little more beautiful in soccer than the reverse pass. Everybody's eyes are going one way, and the genius on the ball reverses direction, cutting through the defense.

Aim: Use a rondo to deliver the opportunity for a reverse pass.

Objectives:

- Keep possession by passing across a grid.
- Reverse a pass to a teammate.

Organisation:

- 20 x 20 m grid
- 6 v 3 players in the grid plus 4, one on each side of the grid.

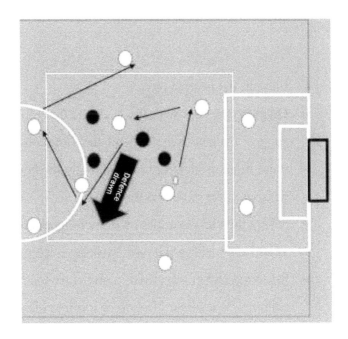

Operation of Drill:

- Play begins with one of the players on the edge of a grid passing to any of their teammates.
- The ball is passed to keep possession.
- When the opportunity presents, a player seeks to reverse the direction of play by pulling the pass to a player on the outside of the grid.
- The drill continues.
- Use the usual methods of rotating defenders and players on the outside.

Key Skills:

- Playing the reverse pass:
- ➢ Disguise the pass with the eyes and body movement to suggest the pass will continue the direction of play.
- ➢ Plant the non-kicking foot and angle the body as though passing in the expected direction.
- ➢ Swing the kicking foot at a tighter angle, and pull the ball slightly in making the pass, striking it later than normal.
- ➢ Since the passer's feet will come close together, it is sometimes necessary to hop or jump to maintain balance.
- ➢ The best reverse passes are for players to run on to. Therefore, the wide players on the grid edge should be on the move.

Development:

- Reduce the number of players on the outside to 3, taking away the player on the rearmost line of the grid.
- Add a goal and a keeper, and the receiver attempts to score.
- Defensive players can leave the grid once the reverse pass is received and attempt to close down the shot.

Fifty-Five (Drill): Rondo match

Aim: Practise skills in a match situation.

For the passing drills we have looked at in the last couple of chapters, we would recommend a full small, sided game, with 7 v 5. This should create sufficient opportunity to practise the skills and techniques covered, but enough opposition to make it difficult.

Fifty-Six (Coaching Strategy): Rondo Matches

It is always good to put into a match situation the skills that have been practised. However, once the sides become too big, or the numbers are even, chances to practise the skills or techniques become limited.

By playing a rondo styled match, it is possible to find a half way house between the two objectives. It is up to the coach how to organise this, but play the game competitively, with two goals. 7 v 4, for example, will give plenty of opportunity for the weighted side to create the space to try moves. 7 v 6 is much harder, and will move the game closer to real match situations.

Fifty-Seven (Coaching Tactic): Doing the Obvious

As coach, we will be clear what the objective of any match practice might be. This is not always apparent to the players – especially younger ones. Stating the obvious is always important, because what is obvious to one is a complete mystery to another.

Key Points from Chapter

We have looked at several drills and tactics to deliver the final, decisive pass. These have built on some of the more general passing points from the previous chapter.

We have concentrated on passing through lines, crossing from wide, and reverse passing to fool the defense.

The key message to take away is that variety really is the spice of life when it comes to soccer. As Liverpool found a decade ago, a tactical approach which is singular and inflexible does not deliver results. Using several different ways of breaking down a defense is far more likely to work. That variety can be produced within a strategic framework of, say, fast, short passing. The more confident players are at playing a variety of passes, and the more familiar a team is with the way it plays, the more likely it is to win.

Rondo drills will help to deliver that success.

The Defense: Playing Out from the Back and the High Press

We have talked already about the evolution of tactics towards playing out from the back, a possession-based game which has emerged thanks to increasing skills and techniques of defensive players. Here, as elsewhere, when the professional game leads, the amateur levels follow.

From there, came the high press among whose early exponents were Jurgen Klopp at Dortmund and which he then took on to Liverpool.

So, in this chapter we will firstly look at how coaches can use rondo drills to help defenders play out from the back, and then how that first line of defense sans first line of attack, the high press, can also be developed through rondo drills.

Fifty-Eight (Coaching Strategy): Establishing the Principle

Confidence, technique and the willingness to accept mistakes. These are the key criteria to playing out from the back. When a striker or advanced midfielder loses the ball, it is annoying. When a defender does the same, it may be a goal that results. That is a risk that players, coaches, supporters – all parties in fact - must be prepared to take.

The other principle to establish at a club level is to begin this tactic from an early age. Which, if we think about it, makes sense. Young children cannot kick the ball long distances in any case, so passing the ball out will lead to success in the end.

Warning: Do not let watching parents tell you anything else. Short term wins are nothing compared to long term development.

Fifty-Nine (Coaching Strategy): Reinforcing the Principle:

Hopefully, this is a point we do not need to reiterate, but just in case…

While we have a couple of drills here to help teams play the ball out from the back, those fine skills of touch, variety of passing and awareness which are crucial to playing the ball out in potentially dangerous situations are built up using regular basic rondo drills such as we covered earlier in the book.

Sixty (Drill): Coming short

Aim: To encourage midfielders to come short to support play and pass wide.

Objectives:

- Midfielder comes short.
- Midfielder plays the ball wide.
- Wide players push wider.
- Possession is retained.

Organisation:

- 15 x 15 m grid.
- 5 v 2 + 1 players.
- Cone 10 m in advance of the grid with the spare players (the midfielder) starting here.

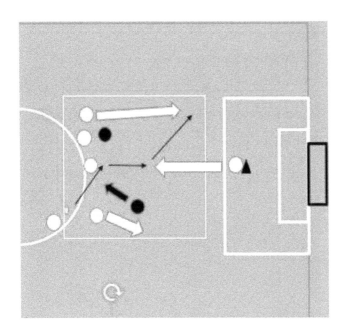

Operation of Drill:

- Play begins with a pass from a player at the base of the grid. (In the match situation, this would usually be the keeper).
- Players retain possession in normal rondo style.
- Meanwhile, the midfielder comes towards the grid.

- As he reaches the grid, the player in possession plays the ball into him or her, and immediately the two widest players push wide outside the grid and advance.
- The midfielder plays a first time pass wide.
- The midfielder jogs back to the cone, and the wide player has a free pass back into the grid, before both wide players re-join the grid.
- Play continues with the midfielder repeating his run to come short.

Key Skills:

- Ball into midfielder's feet must be on ground and firm.
- Midfielder plays a first time pass wide, usually this will be an instep pass swept wide.
- Players take the pass on the half turn so they can turn both ways and have a good idea of pressure.

Development:

- Shrink the playing area to put more pressure on the touch.

Sixty-One (Technique): Delivery from the keeper

The keeper should practice several ways of delivering the ball to the first defender, this is because she will receive the ball in various ways, and under differing amounts of pressure.

Methods include rolling out from arm into a central defender, or to the close full back; bowling out throws to wide full backs; first time and two touch passing with both feet; chipped passing played wide and over a pressuring player to a wide full back.

Sixty-Two (Drill): Playing Out from the back half pitch

Aim: Keep possession from keeper to half-way line. Unusually for a rondo style drill, there is quite a lot of space in this drill.

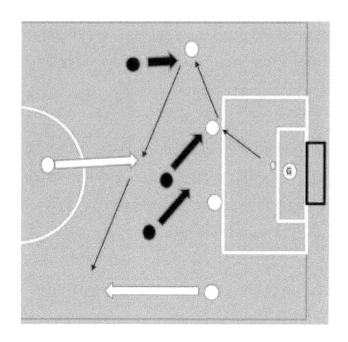

Objectives:

- Keep possession by playing one or two touch passes.
- Get the ball wide so the full backs can advance up the pitch.
- Pass or dribble under control past the half way line.
- Move to support teammates and create easy passing options – triangles!

Organisation:

- Half pitch.
- 6 v 3 players, including a goalkeeper.
- Be prepared to draw defenders in, thus creating more space for teammates.

Operation of Drill:

- Play begins with the goal keeper.
- Full backs are wide. Central defenders are split. Midfielder starts on the half way line.
- Defence must try to prevent progress by any legal means they can.
- Coach will instruct the first pass, to compensate for the lack of defenders.
- The ball should be played around until the opportunity arises to get it wide to a full back in space, who then dribbles or passes forward over the half way line.

Key Skills:

- Patience! Clearly, the normal skills of control, passing, communication etc are crucial, but the team playing out should not attempt to force the ball forwards.
- Be prepared to pass back to the keeper as a spare player and reset.
- Keep moving.
- The decisive pass will often be the midfielder dropping short, and either playing wide or playing a one-two.

Development:

- Increase numbers.

Sixty-Three (Drill): Practising the One Two

We mentioned the one-two in the last drill. In playing out from the back this will often involve the full back playing the ball into the midfielder, who is running back and coming short. The midfielder lays the ball off for the full back.

Aim: Be successful at delivering a one-two

Objectives:

- Pass along the ground and move forwards at speed.
- Receive the pass on the half turn.
- Lay off with a first touch, usually with the outside of the boot.
- Cover the pass in case it is intercepted.

Organisation:

- 15 x 5 m grids. Several can be set up.
- Three minimum attackers and one defender
- One attacker on each side of the grid, one in the middle.

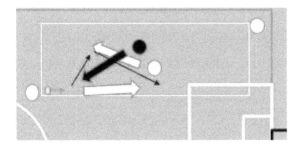

Operation of Drill:

- Attackers split at either end of the grid, on opposite corners.
- Defender starts in the middle of the grid.
- Defender becomes active when non ball 'midfielder' passes them coming for the short pass from the full back.
- Midfielder advances towards the end where the full back is situated.
- When defender becomes active, he or she heads towards the full back, aiming to cut off the dribble.
- Full back passes inside to the midfielder, using the instep, and sprints on.
- Midfielder takes the pass on the half turn and lays it off first time with the outside of the foot to the full back.
- Full back dribbles on and passes to next player ready to go.
- Midfielder joins the back of the other line and next player goes.

Key Skills:

- Firm but sympathetic instep pass.

- Firm pass with outside of foot.
- Midfielder half turns with same shoulder leading as foot which will play the ball.
- Knock the pass firmly ahead of the full back.

Development:

- Encourage two touch passing.
- Let players try different types of passing.

Sixty-Four (Tactic): Encourage Variety

Whilst playing out from the back is a good Coaching Strategy, as with other aspects of soccer, variety leads to greater success. Try other ways of moving the ball up field to allow a bit of extra time when the play out from the back is used.

Sixty-Five (Tactic): Into the Channels

This is an effective way of getting the ball forward, especially if the team's striker is fast.

The full back plays a long past in behind the opposing full back, causing either this play to turn, or the centre half to be dragged out of position.

Sixty-Six (Drill): Rondo High Press – Winning the Ball Up High

Operating a high press requires a few attributes from our team. There is a much larger area to cover, and our team will be at a numerical disadvantage. This is for two reasons; we can only press high if a team is playing out from the back, or the ball will simply bypass our advanced players through a long ball, which means that the opposition at the very least will have the benefit of their keeper as an extra player. Further, we need to get the balance between pressing with sufficient numbers to have a fair chance of winning the ball, and not over-committing and leaving our own defense vulnerable if our high press is defeated.

On top of this, the area we must defend is much, much larger than if we defend with a low block – that is, we do not press until the opposition reach the half-way line. Therefore, we need extreme physical fitness from our team; it is no surprise that even at a professional level, where that fitness is in place, it is frequently strikers and attacking midfielders who are substituted first. As Pep Guardiola once said: 'I want my players chasing the ball like dogs chase dog bones.' Even a dog will run out of energy in the end.

Linked to this, our players need to know when to press, and when to drop. This is a little less effective, more tiring and likely to leave our own defense exposed than one player pressing while his mates drop back to their own half.

The high press drills are therefore like rondos in reverse. We focus on the defense, on winning the ball back and scoring. Remember, now failure will be a more regular visitor than success – but in terms of a match, when success does knock on the door, the gift it carries is a very, very welcome one.

Please note, in the diagram which follows the BLACK Team is in possession, as they are the defensive team being pressed. The grey dotted line is a pass by WHITE after they have won possession.

Aim: Win the ball.

Objectives:

- Work hard to win the ball.

- Cover and anticipate.
- Play a decisive pass after the ball is won.
- Communicate

Organisation:

- 15 x 15 m grid.
- 5 v 3 players.
- One defender plays as a 'keeper' and must remain on the back line of the grid.
- Force the player in possession to hit a long pass or attempt to beat the high press defender on a 1 v 1.

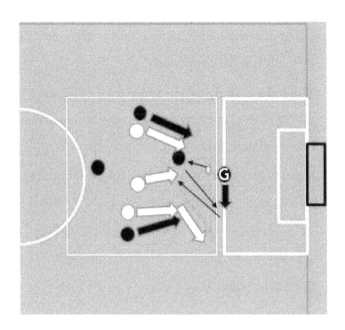

Operation of Drill:

- Play begins with the 'keeper'.
- High press players start on the opposite line and spread across the pitch.
- Nearest player moves to the ball, and jockeys. He or she stays on their toes, half turned, and positioned to prevent a forward pass.
- Other high press players support. They close out the lateral pass, attempting to force the player in possession to

either play the ball long and wide to the other side – a difficult ball, or backwards.

- When the ball is passed backwards, once more the nearest player closes, and teammates support by advancing to cover the next pass.

- If the player in possession can be encouraged to try to beat their high press defender, that is good. Although sometimes they will succeed, the threat is small since they are deep in their own half; sometimes they will fail, and that can present an opportunity to the high press team.

- When the ball is won, the high press team attempt to play one forward pass or two lateral / backwards passes. Then the ball is returned to the keeper and the drill starts again.

- Success is seen in many ways. Mainly, winning the ball and succeeding with the passing movements above; but also, forcing a long pass is a success, as is forcing a backwards pass which allows the press to go higher up again.

Key Skills:

- Body position: we are trying to force the player in possession to play where we want them to – that may be long or attempt to beat us on a 1 v 1, or backwards, or to a player we have isolated as their weakest player. Our body position will help to direct this.

- Communication – the high press players must work as a team.
- Patience – the high press players do not commit to winning the ball until the team in possession make an error – for example a wayward pass or a poor touch. Then they strike.

Development:

- Add a goal for the keeper to defend. On winning possession, the high press team now attempt to score.

Sixty-Seven (Drill): Reverse the Rondo

Aim: Support the attack when winning the ball in a high press.

Objectives:

- Win possession.
- Support the attack.
- Score.

Organisation:

- 20 x 20 m grid.
- 4 v 3 (+ 1 v 3) players, plus keeper.
- Goal.
- Two cones, outside the grid and at the opposite end to the goal. The first grid is 5 m back from the grid, and the three spare high press attackers wait here. The second is 15 m from the grid, and the spare defender waits here.

Operation of Drill:

- Drill begins as in Drill 66.

- When possession is won, the three spare attackers join quickly.

- The spare defender joins.

- The high press team attempt to score.

As in Drill 66, the BLACK team starts in possession.

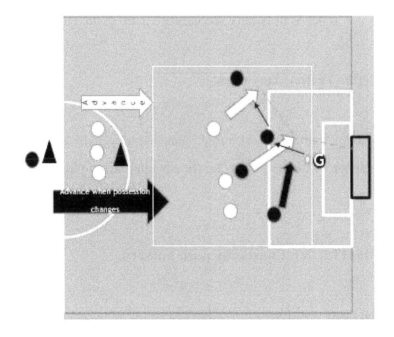

Key Skills:

- Once the ball is won, the high press team must work quickly while they have their numerical advantage.

Development:

- Add a time limit, or maximum number of touches, from winning the ball to getting away a shot at goal. Four touches or twenty seconds are good guides for this.

Sixty-Eight (Tactic): Stay Close

With the high press, encourage pressing players to stay close and work together. When gaps appear, the opposition can play through it and escape.

Sixty-Nine (Tactic): Constantly push forward

The press continues until either the ball is won, or the opposition play through it. Constantly press forward and drop back quickly in the team defensive shape if the opposition do play through the press.

Seventy (Drill): Splendid Isolation

Aim: If the ball cannot be won, isolate the weakest player.

Objectives:

- As with the previous high press drills.
- Another indicator of success is if the 'weak' player ends up in possession.

Organisation:

- Work using any high press rondo drill identified in this section.
- One defender (i.e., the team attempting to play out) wears a bib. This player may ONLY use their weaker foot to play the ball. (Best avoid a two footed player for this drill!)

Operation of Drill:

- As with the drill chosen, the only limitation is that the 'weak' player must be one of the centre halves.

Key Skills:

- Position to force a pass to the 'weak' player.
- Press this player quickly, and support players advance to pick off the weak pass.
- Communicate.

Seventy-One (Tactic): Side By Side

Practise regularly so it becomes second nature that the high press happens in threes or fours. The diagrams below demonstrate ideal pressing positions when the opposition have the ball with the keeper, with the full back and with the centre half.

Seventy-Two (Drill): Rondo drill – Stopping the Midfielder when they Come Short

Aim: Win the ball from the midfield.

Objectives:

- Work together to win the ball off the midfielder.

Organisation:

- Half pitch
- 5 v 3 (1 + 1) players
- Midfielders – the '1 + 1' begin on the half way line.

Operation of Drill:

- Play the ball out from the keeper as before.
- Midfielder for team in possession comes short to receive the ball and sweep it wide.
- High press midfield stays close and prevents the player from turning.

- Pressing players move wider to make the pass to the full back difficult.
- Try to force either a pass back to the keeper, or a mis placed pass.
- Spare pressing player closes down the keeper, forcing a loss of possession or a long kick.
- Drill repeats.

Again, the BLACK team begin in possession.

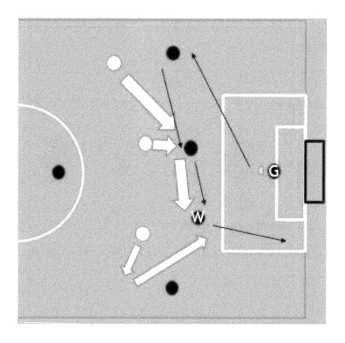

Key Skills:

- Anticipation of the pass.
- Look at the midfielder's body position as they receive the ball.

Seventy-Three (Drill): High Press Game

Play a full 8 v 8 match imposing certain conditions on players to encourage the high press.

Each team has:

One keeper

One defender who must remain in their own half.

Two defenders who can play anywhere.

Two midfielders who can play anywhere

Two attackers who must remain in their opponent's half.

Key Points from the Chapter

Playing out from the back, and consequentially the high press, are here to stay. They enhance the beauty of the game, and both result from the emergence of the rondo, and require it to survive. Fundamentally, defenders become creators, and attackers become ball winners. Both need to practise these new skills. Coaches who neglect to give players such an opportunity do so at their peril.

Combination Passing

Time to return to the core of the rondo – combination passing.

Seventy-Four (Drill): Wall Pass Rondo

Aim: Pass rapidly while moving.

Objectives:

- Change the angle of passing.
- Play round the defender with sharp passing.

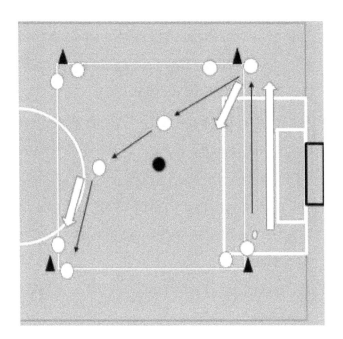

Organisation:

- 15 x 15 m grid with a cone in each corner.
- 10 v 1 players
- Two wall passers and one defender inside the grid, two support passers on each cone.

Operation of Drill:

- Play begins with one of the wall passers passing to any player in a corner.

- This player passes across to either adjacent corner.
- The player who has just passed runs to the cone to which they have just played the ball.
- The receiver plays the ball into the grid, and moves into the grid, taking up a position in space. It is now, briefly, 3 v 1 in the box.
- The wall passer passes to one of his wall pass teammates in the box – this can be the one who has just joined or the other player.
- This player passes to any player on a cone, and then runs to that cone.
- The player on the cone passes to an adjacent cone player and runs to that corner. The play continues.

Key Skills:

- Strong first touch, be it control or pass.
- Firm but accurate pass with the instep.
- Wall passers constantly looking for space away from the defender.

Development:

- Restrict to one touch passing.

Seventy-Five (Drill): Rotations

Aim: Admittedly, this is not strictly a rondo drill, because there is no opposition as such. Except…yourself, and most professionally sportsmen and women admit overcoming their own limitations is one of the biggest challenges a performer faces…

Objectives:

- Concentrate hard on where ball is to be played.
- Sympathetic, accurate first time lay off, controlling the pace of the ball.

Organisation:

- 15 x 15 m grid.
- Cone in each corner.
- 4 players.
- Two balls.

- One attacker on each of three corners of the grid. One attacker in the middle.

In the diagram below, the numbers in the grey circles indicate the other of the passe, the numbers in the black circles indicate the order of the runs.

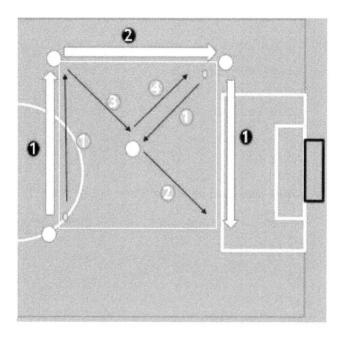

Operation of Drill:

- Play begins with two simultaneous actions.

- The player on the final corner, i.e., the last one where this is a player positioned, passes the ball into the grid player, and runs to the empty corner.
- Meanwhile the player on the first corner passes to the player on the second corner.
- The three players on the outside must run clockwise to the next corner AFTER they have played a pass.
- The grid player plays a pass into the EMPTY corner and turns to receive the next pass.

Key Skills:

- Controlled first time pass.
- Concentration.
- Controlled movement.

Seventy-Six (Drill): Short, Short, Long

Aim: Create space with combination of different lengths of passes.

Note: Numbers in the white movement arrows indicate the order of movement, following a pass and move pattern.

Objectives:

- Keep possession with sharp passing.
- Create space with a longer pass.

Organisation:

- 20 x 15 m grid.
- 4 v 1 player
- One player remains as the wall pass player within the grid.
- Pair of players on one corner.
- Opposite on the long side, the other attacking player.
- One defender begins on other side of grid, and opposite corner to the attacking players.

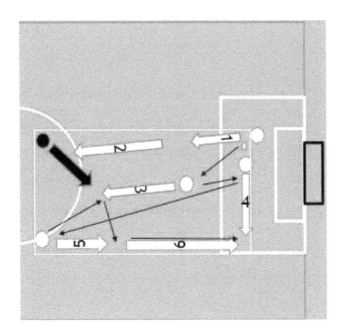

Operation of Drill:

- Play starts in one corner.
- Short pass to the wall player and move.
- Short pass from wall player, either a return pass, or a knock back to player still on the corner.
- Long pass to another end.
- First passer and wall player move down grid, defender tries to disrupt.
- Drill repeated from the other end.

Key Skills:

- Pass and move with one touch football.
- This drill is really aiming to perfect skills of passing, movement, communication and touch learned earlier.

Seventy-Seven (Tactic): Slowing Down the Opposition

As good as our team might become at combination passing, we might also find ourselves on the other end of the strategy. A good tactic to counter combination passing is to slow down the opposition by dropping deeper and closing down space in the key areas of the pitch. Spectacular passing is good to watch, but if it happens outside the final third, it rarely causes damage. Drop into two banks of four, with the spare strikers dropping in when a player is pulled out to pressure. Strike hard and with pace the opposition make a mistake.

Seventy-Eight (Drill): Through the Gate

Aim: Use one and two touch passing combinations to create space for a precision passing.

Objectives:

- Pass the ball quickly to create the space for a key pass.
- Show teamwork awareness by being in position to receive the pass.

Organisation:

- Large, 20 x 20 m grid.
- Inside grid, four 2 x 2 m gates (shown in the diagram by the short dotted lines), 5 m from the edge of the grid, and offset.
- 6 x 3 players
- Passing team attempt to create the space to pass the ball through a gate. To be successful, the ball must be controlled by a teammate the other side of the gate.

- The attacking team cannot 'score' twice in a row through the same gate.

- The defense score by simply passing the ball through the grid.

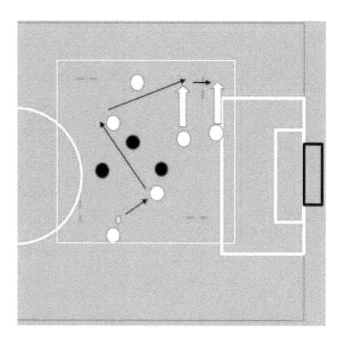

Operation of Drill:

• Once set up, this is a simple drill, characterised by fast passing.

Key Skills:

- Communication to get into position for pass.
- Seeing the picture – players form a picture of how a move is developing.
- Other key skills are the ones associated with one and two touch passing – i.e., control, body position and so forth.

Development:

- Remove two of the gates.
- Play 4 v 4, with two 'spare' players, wearing bibs, who always join in with the team in possession.

Seventy-Nine (Coaching Strategy): Keep It Light and Active

Some of the more recent drills have become complicated. This is fine, but coaches must be aware of keeping up the pace of the session, especially with younger players. Have drills already set up, or interchange complicated ones with simple, fast action.

For coaches fortunate enough to have an 'assistant', have different drills operating simultaneously, around which the players can rotate.

Key Points on Combination Passing

As players improve so drills can become more complicated. Remember to retain the fun in the game. We play because we enjoy it. Nevertheless, fast combination passing wins games. It creates chances and splits defences. Encourage our teams to develop combination passing in the final third, where the biggest danger can be caused...and losing possession is unlikely to result in a direct threat on our team's goal.

Transition

Of all aspects of the modern game, perhaps transition has become the most important. This is a good thing, since transitions lead to counter attacks, and seeing a winger bursting past the last defender, or a midfielder playing a precision pass, or a centre forward powering through are among the most important aspects of soccer.

Eighty (Drill): Twin Grids

Aim: Transition quickly to attack.

Objectives:

- Break quickly and support teammates on transition.
- Work back to protect the defense when possession is lost.
- Score.

Organisation:

- Two 10 x 10 m grid, with a goal just beyond each.
- 10 m gap between the grids.

- 3 attackers and 2 defenders in each grid. 1 player from each side in the central area. 1 keeper for each team.

Operation of Drill:

- Ball begins with one team in the central area.
- Player passes or dribbles unopposed into attacking grid. Player is permitted in the attacking grid, making this a 4 v 2 rondo.
- Team attempts to score.
- When possession is lost in any way, there is a free pass into the space between the grids.
- One of the attacking players – it does not have to be the original midfielder – moves back into the central space. He or she may not attempt to win possession.
- The drill repeats the other way.

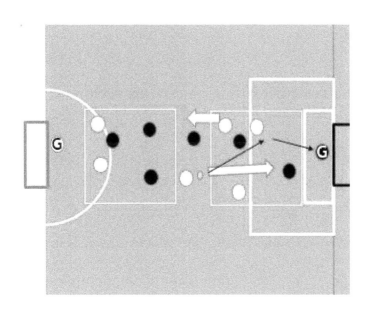

Key Skills:

- Speed of movement on transition is key.

Development:

- Allow opposition in the defensive grid and middle space to make the game more match-like.

Eighty-One (Drill): Change on Transition

Aim: Make use of numerical advantage of transition.

Objectives:

- Keep possession once it is won on transition.

Organisation:

- 10 x 10 m grid.
- 2 v 2 players plus 2 to support whichever side is in possession.

Operation of Drill:

- A very straightforward rondo where players within the grid aim to keep possession.
- Players, marked by their bibs, support whichever team is in possession. They swap sides, therefore, when possession changes.

Key Skills:

- As with other drills, this drill works well as a warm up for the fuller game drill explained in drill eighty-four.

Eighty-Two (Coaching Strategy): The Beauty of Bibs

A great way to turn almost any drill into one which can help to develop skills in transition is to turn the excess members of the attacking team into 'bibbed' players – ones who will always work with the side in possession.

This allows quicker transition when the ball is lost, and is realistic to the game situation when, on winning the ball, defenders do indeed become attackers. Thus, when the two defenders take possession, rather than simply swapping the defenders and waiting for this to happen, the bibbed strikers change sides, reversing the offense and defense

Eighty-Three (Tactic): Formation in Transition

With older players particularly, say from Under 12s upwards, begin to introduce the tactic of how to break on transition.

It is important to be prepared for a quick break the other way if our team loses the ball again quickly. Players need to think on their feet, deciding whether they are in a best position to break forward to support the attack, or hold in case they are needed in defense.

The following match drill helps players to develop this sense of tactical awareness.

Eighty-Four (Drill): On the Break

Aim: Win the game

Objectives:

- Score goals.
- Break quickly on transition, utilising our extra players.

Organisation:

- Full pitch
- 9 v 9 including goalkeepers + 2 players who play with the team in possession. (Younger age groups who play smaller sided games can play with smaller numbers.)

- Normal game, except when possession changes, the spare two players change to play with the side who have the ball.

Operation of Drill:

- Normal match other than the transition rule above.

Key Skills:

- Judge whether to break forward or hold on transition.
- Coach stops the game regularly to explore the decision making that has taken place.

Development:

- This drill can be played indoors using 4 v 4 + 1.

Eighty-Five (Coaching Strategy): Small Sided v Large Sided drills

Those of us who have coached younger age groups will be familiar with the question – 'Do we have a match at the end?'

Why not? Sessions are about fun, and there is something enjoyable, collegiate almost, about the full sided game. It does little harm, and maybe even helps players understand the perspective of the bigger pitch and increased levels of opposition.

Unfortunately, what it does not do is to help individual players improve their touch and technique. That is because where there are more players about, the chances of a touch for any individual are reduced. This is pure maths, if 1000 touches occur during a match practice, in an eleven a side game, that is 50 touches per person on average, excluding keepers. If we cut the numbers to six a side, that average increases to just over 80 per player.

More than that, the quality of the touch is reduced since players have less time and space on the ball. That is why the rondo is such a good drill – there is huge opportunity for touches, but the presence of some opposition adds an element of jeopardy, making the drill more serious than an unopposed drill.

We are not against the full sided drill or practice, but like the best whiskey, they should be tasted in extreme moderation.

From this chapter we can take away the following key points:

- On transition break quickly and purposefully.
- Do not over commit.
- Develop excellent vision, one and two touch play.
- Use rondo drills to create transition drills which are transferable to the match situation.
- Use small-sided drills far more often than large, sided ones.

Key Points from this Chapter

- The importance of transition in the game cannot be expressed strongly enough.
- The use of neutral players is an effective way of carrying out rondo drills.
- Inevitably, transition activities require larger numbers of players. Remember that drills with more players equate to fewer touches on the ball.

Using Rondos to Develop Players

As we have seen, rondo drills do develop our players. They develop virtually all elements of a soccer player's arsenal. We can take it a stage further. Take a look at the rondo below – it should seem familiar.

Eighty-Six (Drill): Pass and Move

Aim: Improve communication. (NOT, as we would expect, improve first touch, or movement, or passing…)

Objectives:

- Keep possession by passing across a circle.
- Receive the ball in the correct body position to make the next pass.
- Keep possession by passing with one or two touches.
- Move to support a teammate…
- Yes, we have seen this before. Absolutely crucial skills for a soccer player, but own objective here is to *improve communication.* Anything else is a bonus.

Organisation:

- Circle with 15m diameter.
- 5 v 1 players
- Attackers around the edge of the circle. Defender in the middle.
- When possession is lost the player responsible swaps with the defender.
- Very straightforward. Not that this does not make the drill valuable, but in the operation stage below, we see how the coach very simply tweaks the drill to make it suit her purpose.

Operation of Drill:

- Play begins with the player in possession calling the name of one of their teammates.
- The teammate indicates where she wants the pass played.
- That player then runs to the space to which she has pointed, as the player plays the pass.
- Passer runs to the spot where they have just played the ball.

- The drill continues.
- Good passes must be encouraged by teammates.
- If the defender wins the ball, they must be congratulated.

Key Skills:

- Players are communicating now in two ways, both important.
- Specific instruction to help ensure the passer and receiver are both of the same mind.
- General encouragement which helps to raise players' self-esteem and therefore confidence.

Development:

- That drill can be adapted for different areas we wish to develop in our players. For example…
- Movement is predictable: pass and run to a space.
- Jimmy and Julie are too one footed: they must use their weaker foot.
- Develop disguise: look to one spot for the pass, so the defender sees, and pass to another.

Eighty-Seven (Coaching Strategy): Adapting Rondos

Coaches can make more use of the rondos explained in this book by simply adapting them to make their own particular goal for a drill the main focus. Since most rondo drills use the same basic tenets – an overload of attacking players, small areas, quick passing, aiming to retain possession, decision making, fun – as coach we can decide what we want to achieve, explain it (briefly!) to our players, and get underway.

The goal is reinforced by the coach's instructions and comments.

Try having a look at some of the rondos in this book, and set a slightly adapted goal for them, and see how easy it is to manipulate them to achieve the goal.

Eighty-Eight (Coaching Strategy): Some Rondo Theory

When we decide how to use rondos to develop our players, we can apply some simple theory to how they are used.

We can divide rondos into three levels. These are:

Level One: Basic Skills and Techniques: Here the rondos used are working on the key skills needed for soccer players, such as touch, passing, communication, movement and so forth. These rondos have as their basic element the overload, a small area such as a grid or circle, and the aim of keeping possession. Although they are simple, that does not mean that they are not useful. Watch the warm up for a professional game, and this type of rondo will often be used even with players at the very top of the sport.

Level Two: Team Shape Rondos: Here we see rondos used to help players hold their shape on the pitch. Mostly, this is about micro shape, i.e., the positions that are adopted in small phases of the game. For example, being in the position to receive the next pass, or for the defense positioning to prevent a pass. Although macro positioning, or formation (e.g., 5, 4, 1 out of possession) forms a part of this, it is the specific localised positioning on the pitch that the rondos mostly help to develop. Examples include using a rondo to create the space for a key pass or using a rondo to improve play out from the back.

Level Three: Match Play Rondos or Transition Rondos: These are rondos which help to develop players in transition stages of the game.

These transitions include winning possession, turning defense into attack, creating chances by playing through the midfield. They are typically played in larger areas and involve more players, although the key element of the overload remains. The rondos in this book which included bibbed players who switch teams depending on which side has possession are examples of this kind of rondo.

As coach, we can decide which element of the game our players need to work on and use rondos which satisfy this.

Eighty-Nine (Tactic): Which Skills remain at the Core of the Soccer Player?

In the coaching strategy above, we can quickly deduce that the levels increase in complexity. Therefore, it seems reasonable that we would use Level One rondos with younger teams, Level Two as we begin to bring in tactical elements to our team play and Level Three when we are lucky enough to be coaching a team both talented AND experienced.

This is only partly true. If we neglect basic skills with talented players, those skills will begin to fade. After all, if the great Barcelona team of the late 2000s' decade work with Level One rondos, then probably so should our U15 team who are top of the league. Conversely, while we will spend much more time with our U8s on acquiring basic skills, this age is very able to see how a game might develop, and how their role can change in different circumstances. The days of 'I'm a defender and so I don't cross the halfway line…' or 'Why should I defend, I'm a forward?' are, fortunately, long gone. Level Two and Level Three rondos, adapted for the age and ability of the players, will help to ensure that they do not return.

Ninety (Drill) Level One Rondo: Position the Defender

Aim: Help the defensive players to perfect their body positions.

Objectives (for the defense):

- Close down on the half turn.
- Work as a team to close space.
- Force the pass to where you want to go.
- Move to support your teammate when the attacking side successfully play round you.

Organisation:

- 15 m diameter circle.

- 5 v 2 players.

- Attackers around the outside, defense in the middle.

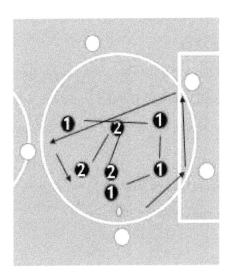

Operation of Drill:

- Offense keep possession in usual manner. Coach can set limits on the number of touches depending on the ability of the players.

- First defender closes down on the half turn, body positioned to allow a pass in only one direction.

- Chest of defender broadly pointing towards the direction of pass.
- Second defender, supports behind, again on half turn They spin and close the receiver, again directing where the pass should be made. If the receiver errs, they can try to make the tackle or interception.
- First defender closes the anticipated direction of the next pass.
- They may be able to intercept that pass or tackle the next receiver if the pass is wayward. Since that passer was under pressure, this may be the case.

Here we have numbered the defenders to show their movement around the grid to force the final pass to fail.

Key Skills:

- Defense communicate and work together.
- Quite quickly, the defenders will know how their teammate is going to position themselves.
- Body position of defense.
- Patience. Do not dive in until the defender is sure that they can win the ball.

- Decision making.

Development:

- Change the grid shape to a square. This makes it harder to close down the spaces.

Ninety-One (Drill) Level Two Rondo: Split the Defense for a Through Pass

Aim: Play a pass between defenders.

Objectives:

- Pass quickly to draw defense out of their preferred position.
- Communicate and feint passes to spread defense further.
- When space is there, play the through pass.
- Move along the line of the grid.

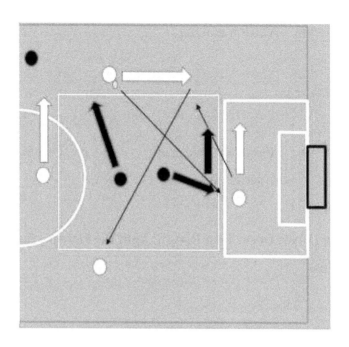

Organisation:

- 10 x 10 m grid.
- 4 v 2 players.
- Attacker each have one side of the grid which they can, and should, move along.

214

Operation of Drill:

- Defense aims to stay together to prevent the through pass. (It is better defense to make opponents play round you than through you.)
- Fast, one or two touch passing, moves defense around quickly.
- Movement and communication causes defense to split.
- Through pass is played.

Key Skills:

- On top of the normal, key, skills and techniques which all rondos help to develop, patience is required.
- Feinting to pass one way but passing the other will also cause confusion to the defense.

Development:

- Add extra players.

Ninety-Two (Drill) Level Three Rondo: Creating Shooting Opportunities

Aim: Use fast passing and movement to create the space for a shot at goal.

Objectives:

- Pass swiftly to draw defense.
- Play the key pass to open opportunity for shot.
- Accurate and effective shooting.

Organisation:

- Half pitch.
- 5 v 3 players plus keeper.
- Goal.

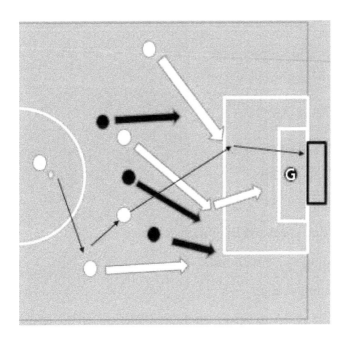

Operation of Drill:

- Start on the halfway line.
- Pass short and long (not too long!) to draw defense out of position.
- Move play to one side of pitch to draw defense.
- Make a run from midfield to either draw defense further out of position or, if the defense does not respond, to be in position to shoot when the ball is received.
- Move away into space.
- Key pass.

217

- Shoot.
- Follow in for rebounds.

Key Skills:

- Timing of runs.
- Patience.
- Passing short and long with accuracy.
- Finding space with runs.
- Communication.
- Shooting. Aim across goal, hard and low where appropriate.
- Players follow in shot (defense and attack) for rebounds.

Development:

- Move to a whole pitch game.
- Create the overload by having some players who must stay in a particular half, with others who can move between halves when their team is in possession.

Key Points from the Chapter

In this chapter we have seen that all rondos help to develop players, but they can be tweaked to focus particularly on specific skills that the coach identifies as needing special attention.

By dividing rondo drills into three levels, coaches can determine into which level the skill, tactic or technique they wish to develop best fits, and find or create rondos accordingly.

Small Sided Rondo Games

Everybody loves a game. We wouldn't play soccer if we did not have a competitive element to us. Here are some small-sided rondo drills which can have an element of 'goal scoring' to them. In each case, the skills developed are the same, key ones, as always. However, the thrill of 'winning' is added.

Ninety-Three (Drill): Two v One and Score

Aim: Pass and Shoot

Objectives:

- Play a one-two to get into a shooting position.
- Shoot and score.

Organisation:

- Penalty area
- 8(divided into four groups of 2) v 1 players plus a goalkeeper.

- Defender begins on penalty spot. Player one on edge of D, player two on corner of D and penalty area.
- One point for shot on target.
- Three points for a goal.
- Total up team scores.

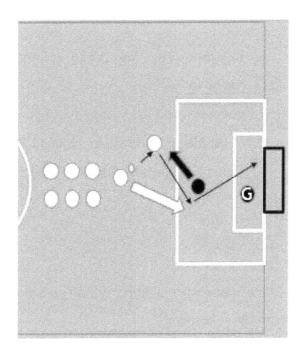

Operation of Drill:

- Player one passes and runs into space.
- Defender must close ball – if not, player one can shoot.

- When defender closes ball, pass into space.
- Player two shoots.
- Next pair goes.
- On each pairs' second attempt, swap roles.

Key Skills:

- Key pass – open hips to pass in front of teammate to run on to.
- Shoot low and hard across the goal.
- Other player chases in for rebound.
- Defender chases back to clear rebound.

Development:

- Start from deeper and play drill to give player a chance to dribble at keeper.

Ninety- Four (Drill): Keep It Going

This is a super-fast drill, great fun to play, which helps develop muscle memory for positioning. It is complicated but once the players

have the idea, they will love it. To make it more into a rondo drill, add
a defender.

Aim: Keep the drill going for as long as possible.

Here, the runs and players are numbered to make their movements clearer.

Objectives:

- Keep possession with fast, one touch passing.
- See how long possession can be kept before the drill breaks down. Or count the passes for even more fun (especially for younger players).

Organisation:

- 6 x 6 m square on a pentagon. Player on the pentagon corner plays in the same way as everybody else.
- 6 v 0 players
- One player in centre of grid, remainder on cones around outside.

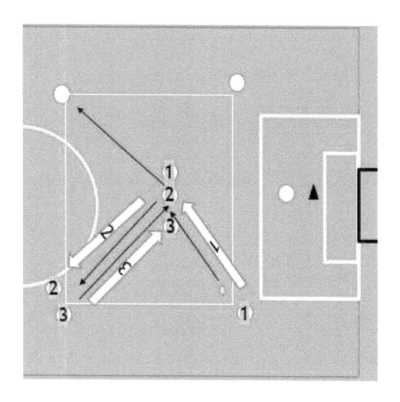

Operation of Drill:

- Play begins with one player passing to the player in the middle.
- This player then runs to the middle.
- Receiver opens hips to play a first-time pass to next player along.
- Receiver runs to this cone.
- Ball played back into the middle and so on.

224

Key Skills:

- Weight of pass.
- Open hips to pass in front of receiver.
- Movement.

Ninety-Five (Drill): Escape from Alcatraz

This is a drill which rewards the defense. As can be seen, it is a standard 4 v 2 rondo, but the fun comes when possession is won by the defense.

Aim: Dribble out of the prison.

Objectives:

- Offense must keep possession.
- Players work on transition.

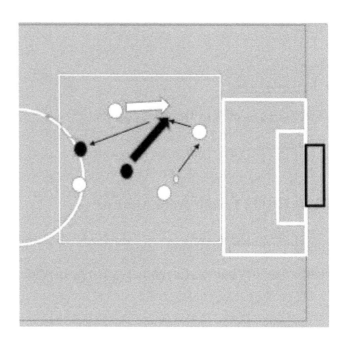

Organisation:

- 10 x 10 m square.
- 4 v 2 players. Work this with three teams of two. Each team has a session, say two minutes, in defense. This is when they can score points. The other four players join up as one team to keep possession.

Operation of Drill:

- The attackers try to retain possession.

- When possession is won by the defense, they must dribble out of the grid. Passing is allowed.
- Point for each time they successfully dribble out.
- If attackers win the ball back, play continues as before.

Key Skills:

- Responding to transition.

Development:

- A goal can be added outside the grid, and rather than dribble out the defense attempts to get a shot away on winning possession. Again, passing and dribbling are allowed.

The key point from this chapter is that everybody enjoys playing games, and soccer must be about fun. However, from a progress perspective, by definition match practice involves more players than most drills. Therefore, touches per player are reduced. This can be countered with carefully prepared rondo match drills.

Preparing a Rondo Based Training Session

A brief chapter now on planning.

Ninety-Six (Coaching Strategy): Identifying the Aims of a Session

A soccer coach is a teacher. One who has the benefit of a class who are very committed to their learning, and who can teach a wonderful subject. But, like a teacher, it is not just about the delivery of coaching.

A coach who works without a plan will come unstuck in the end. They will run out of original drills and will find themselves scratching around for things to do. Inevitably, when this happens, coaching drops away and more and more time is spent on large, sided games and activities which occupy rather than develop our players.

Ideally, planning works on three levels.

At the broadest are the season aims. These most likely include general objectives about developing skills and techniques, along with tactical awareness. Secondly there will be physical aims, mostly around fitness and the general benefits being physically fit brings. Finally, and just as importantly, there will be mental health objectives. This will centre around self-esteem, confidence, team work, friendship, confidence, resilience and so forth.

At the next level should be some kind of broad plan. This may well be part of a whole club philosophy; it will look at skill development in more detail, for example.

Then comes the detailed plan for each session, which draws on those wider objectives and assessment of recent sessions and matches. So, for example, our long-term plan might state that a particular week looks at movement off the ball. Our assessment might tell us that we need to also work on first touch. Thus, we can develop drills which work on both objectives. At this level, we might also identify individual targets, and look to focus some time on individual players.

Which is, of course, why rondo drills are so effective because they do develop multiple skills.

Ninety-Seven (Coaching Strategy): Do I really need to Write It Down?

There is a simple answer to this question. Who are we writing our plan down for? If it is for a third party, for somebody to see what we are doing, then no. If they are that interested, they can come and watch. But if we are writing it down for ourselves, it is because it will make the session more useful for our players, then the answer is yes. Brief notes will be useful.

But they are notes for ourselves. If we know exactly which resources we need for a particular drill, why write it down? If we might forget that we need to get the goals moved for a drill, and this will then slow down the session, then we should make a note.

If we will remember everything from the session and know exactly how we will assess that to inform planning for next week, then no, we do not need to make notes. But honestly, we will probably forget something, so having a sheet on which we can jot notes will help Similarly, if we know exactly what drills we will be doing, plus a couple of spares if timing or numbers dictate, then that is fine. As we become more experienced, we probably need to write less. On the other hand, newer coaches, or any who are introducing untried, challenging, skills and techniques will benefit from having some notes which hold the details of the session. Then our minds can focus on how to best help our players acquire that tricky skill or tactic. The paper will hold the mundane details, and our minds can focus on higher levels of thinking and coaching.

So, yes, mostly we should write down our plans. But in a way that helps ourselves. Since we wrote the plan, we need only key words or phrases to remind us of what we are doing.

Ninety-Eight (Plan): Sample Session Plan (1)

We are including a couple of broad plans as guides. Each assumes a one-hour training session played across half a full sized pitch, with the other half of the pitch used to coach another team in our club. This session assumes one coach and twelve players. The coach has access to balls, cones, goals and bibs.

Aim of session: Improve first touch.

Plan:

5 minutes: Greet players and send off to work on a 3 v 1 warm up as they arrive.

10 minutes: Pass and move rondo warm up. Two touches, focus on first touch.

10 minutes: Competitive Rondo: 3 v 3 + 2 + keepers. Bibs for 2, who will play with team in possession. Position coach to watch game and also work with Player A and Player B on technique for first touch, since they are struggling with this.

5 minutes: Plenary with drinks break – what do we know about first touch?

10 minutes: Two rondo drills: 4 v 2 keep possession, and 3 v 2 plus a keeper and goal. Five minutes on each then swap.

15 minutes: 7 v 5 games. Three short games, five minutes each, swap teams every five minutes.

5 minutes; Cool down, 10 v 2 rondo in a circle.

Ninety-Nine (Plan): Session Plan 2

This time we assume that the coach has an assistant (ASST), allowing for smaller drills each with a coach watching closely.

Aim: Improve short passing

5 minutes: Greet arrivals, while ASST operates 3 v 1 passing rondo.

10 minutes: Divide group into two, one touch passing drill in pentagon shape.

10 minutes: Divide group into two, short, short, long passing drill.

10 minutes: Passing through the middle drill, splitting defense.

5 minutes: Plenary on passing, drinks break.

5 minutes: ASST works with Players A and B on technique for passing with outside of the foot. Remainder 2 v 1 passing and shooting drill.

10 minutes: 4 v 4 + 2 (who support team in possession) game. Coach focusses on short passing. ASST on other forms of passing.

5 minutes: Cool down, 10 v 2 one touch passing in circle.

Our *key point* from this brief chapter is that planning is almost as important as delivery when it comes to coaching.

Conclusion

We have shown the value of the rondo, although nothing is perfect, either in life or in soccer. Rondos do carry risks. Unless carefully handled, they can reduce confidence. It is important that being made a defender after a control or passing error is not seen as a punishment. Practically, a lot of space is needed for rondos because they tend to involve small groups, and therefore multiple paying areas need to be in place. It is best, especially with younger players, to call rondo drills by a variety of names. Even though each drill is valuable and varied, just hearing the word 'rondo' can make younger players feel that they are just doing the same drills over and again.

In many ways they will be, so we need to disguise the fact.

But with care, rondos really do develop players, and have taken coaching forwards in leaps and bounds over the past decade.

One Hundred (Coaching Strategy): A Reminder of Why Coaches Should Use Rondos

It's simple. They deliver key skills and technique; they replicate some of the pressure of real match situation, but in a way which allows intense practice of the skill on which the team is working. They are fun.

For these reasons, rondos work. One of the greatest teams in the history of football, the Barcelona sides of the first decade of the twenty-first century built their play them and used rondos to deliver their philosophy. If it is good enough for Cruyff, for Guardiola, for Messi, for Xavi, for Iniesta...and then good enough for top coaches across the world to instil the rondo philosophy in their own coaching...surely it is good enough for us.

Happy coaching. Remember, have fun, then our players will as well.

If you liked this book, we have a few more soccer books that we recommend below:

It's a Numbers Game: A look into how numbers affect the game of soccer.

<u>Soccer Smarts for Kids</u>: A collection of drills that are useful for kids starting to play soccer

<u>Soccer IQ</u>: A great look into what makes a good soccer player

The end... almost!

Reviews are not easy to come by.

As an independent author with a tiny marketing budget, I rely on readers, like you, to leave a short review on Amazon.

Even if it's just a sentence or two!

So if you enjoyed the book, please browse to the product page and leave a review as shown below:

I am very appreciative for your review as it truly makes a difference.

Thank you from the bottom of my heart for purchasing this book and reading it to the end.

Lightning Source UK Ltd.
Milton Keynes UK
UKHW020625200921
390889UK00010B/266